I0015169

Network Marketing

How to Become a Network Marketing Rock Star

(The Secret to Building a Successful Team While Creating Passive Income)

Gustavo Gilbert

Published By **Andrew Zen**

Gustavo Gilbert

Network Marketing: How to Become a Network Marketing Rock Star (The Secret to Building a Successful Team While Creating Passive Income)

ISBN   978-1-7779561-5-8

Legal & Disclaimer

Table Of Contents

Chapter 1: Building A Winning Mindset

Developing the Right Mindset for Success in Network Marketing, Overcoming Self-Limiting Beliefs, and Setting Achievable Goals

"Your attitude is the foundation upon which your fulfillment in network advertising is built." - Unknown

I welcome you again to the exhilarating global of community advertising and marketing and advertising, wherein achievement starts offevolved offevolved with a winning attitude. In this financial disaster, we're capable of discover the crucial function thoughts-set plays in engaging in success in community advertising and marketing and marketing. We will dive deep into the power of beliefs, the paintings of purpose putting, and the techniques for overcoming self-restricting beliefs. Get equipped to unharness your internal champion and embark on a adventure of personal boom and fulfillment.

The Power of Mindset in Network Marketing

In community advertising, your mindset is the essential trouble differentiator amongst fulfillment and mediocrity. It shapes your mind, attitudes, and moves, in the end figuring out your stage of success. A prevailing mind-set is characterized through way of resilience, positivity, and a burning preference to be successful.

"Your mind-set, now not your flair, will determine your altitude." - Zig Ziglar

Overcoming Self-Limiting Beliefs

"Whether you believe you studied you can otherwise you determined you can't, you are right." - Henry Ford

Self-proscribing beliefs are the invisible limitations that maintain us decrease lower again from attaining our entire capability. These beliefs stem from past research, societal conditioning, or worry of failure. To construct a triumphing attitude, we must perceive and undertaking those self-imposed limitations.

Let's consider an example: Sarah, a community marketer, believes that she is not proper at earnings. This belief creates a intellectual block and forestalls her from coming near possibilities with self perception. By hard this belief and reframing it as an possibility to look at and expand, Sarah can conquer her self-restricting belief and free up her genuine capability.

Setting Achievable Goals

"Goals are dreams with time limits." - Diana Scharf Hunt

Goal placing is a essential trouble of building a prevailing mind-set. Without clear goals, we wander aimlessly and struggle to live endorsed. When putting dreams in community marketing and marketing, it's miles crucial to motive them to Specific, Measurable, Achievable, Relevant, And Time-Bound (SMART).

Let's maintain in mind an instance: John, a network marketer, units a intention to recruit ten new institution contributors within the subsequent 3 months. By putting a selected and time-positive purpose, John can popularity his efforts, tune his development, and have a great time each milestone completed.

Strategies for Building a Winning Mindset

Cultivate Positivity and Gratitude

"Positive wondering will will let you do the whole lot higher than terrible wondering will." - Zig Ziglar

Maintaining a top notch mind-set is crucial for fulfillment in network advertising. Surround your self with uplifting human beings, exercise gratitude day by day, and interest at the opportunities in preference to the worrying conditions. Remember, a superb mind-set attracts exceptional effects.

Continuous Learning and Personal Growth

"Leaders are readers." - Unknown

Network advertising is an ever-evolving agency, and staying beforehand requires a determination to non-save you analyzing. Invest in private improvement, attend education occasions, take a look at books, and attempting to find mentorship from a fulfillment network marketers. Embrace the mind-set of a lifelong learner and watch your achievement bounce.

Visualization and Affirmations

"Your thoughts shape your truth." - Unknown

Visualization is a powerful method utilized by a achievement community marketers to show up their goals. Create a superb highbrow photograph of your preferred effects, interact all of your senses, and immerse your self within the feelings associated with undertaking the ones goals. Coupled with wonderful affirmations, visualization amplifies the electricity of your unconscious thoughts.

Chapter 2: Effective Prospecting Techniques

Strategies for Finding and Approaching Potential Customers and Distributors, Including Online and Offline Prospecting Methods

"Prospecting is the lifeblood of community advertising and marketing. It's the artwork of uncovering diamonds in the tough and transforming them into valuable property." - Unknown

Welcome to the interesting global of prospecting! In this financial catastrophe, we are capable of discover the vital strategies and strategies for efficaciously finding and approaching functionality customers and vendors in community advertising. Whether you're a seasoned community marketer or genuinely starting your journey, mastering the paintings of prospecting is critical for fulfillment. So, permit's dive in and find out the secrets and techniques and strategies to constructing a thriving network.

The Importance of Prospecting in Network Marketing

Prospecting is the spine of network advertising and marketing. It is the gadget of identifying folks that may be interested in your products or company possibility and beginning a communication with them. Without powerful prospecting, your community advertising and marketing organisation will struggle to expand and flourish.

"Prospecting is like mining for gold. The more you dig, the greater treasures you may find out." - Unknown

Finding Potential Customers and Distributors

To construct a a achievement community advertising business enterprise, you have to continuously locate new functionality clients and distributors. Here are some powerful techniques for finding opportunities:

Tap into Your Warm Market

Your heat market consists of your friends, family, pals, and colleagues. Start thru the usage of conducting out to them and sharing your merchandise or agency opportunity. Remember to approach them with professionalism and respect, and be organized to reply their questions.

Attend Networking Events and Trade Shows

Networking sports and exchange indicates offer outstanding possibilities to connect to like-minded people and enlarge your network. Be organized together collectively together with your elevator pitch, engage in huge conversations, and gather contact facts for observe-up.

Utilize Social Media Platforms

Social media structures at the side of Facebook, Instagram, and LinkedIn are powerful equipment for prospecting in current day virtual age. Create a compelling on line presence, percent valuable content cloth, and have interaction alongside facet your target audience. Join relevant agencies and groups to connect to people who share comparable pursuits.

Approaching Potential Customers and Distributors

Once you have got got diagnosed potential prospects, it's miles crucial to approach them in a professional and persuasive way. Here are a few powerful strategies for drawing close potentialities:

Build Relationships and Provide Value

"People do now not care how an entire lot you understand until they understand how a whole lot you care." - Unknown

Take the time to gather proper relationships collectively along with your possibilities. Show a actual interest in their goals and dreams, and offer answers that might add rate to their lives. By specializing in building agree with and presenting rate, you set up a solid basis for long-time period relationships.

Use the Power of Storytelling

"Facts inform, however stories promote." - Unknown

Storytelling is a effective tool for connecting together along with your possibilities on an emotional degree. Share success testimonies, testimonials, and private evaluations that screen the transformational power of your merchandise or corporation possibility. Stories have the functionality to inspire, captivate, and create a experience of opportunity.

Follow Up Consistently

"Fortune is in the follow-up." - Mary Kay Ash

Following up is a important step in the prospecting way. Many potentialities may not be prepared to decide proper now, so it is essential to stay in contact and provide additional records or help as wanted. Consistent take a look at-up demonstrates your dedication and professionalism.

Chapter 3: Effective Communication Skills

Enhancing Communication Skills to Effectively Present Products or Business Opportunities, Handle Objections, and Build Relationships

"Communication is the important issue that unlocks the door to success in community marketing. It's the art work of connecting, influencing, and provoking others." - Unknown

Welcome to the bankruptcy committed to studying powerful verbal exchange talents in network advertising. In this economic destroy, we are able to discover the crucial strategies and strategies for presenting merchandise or commercial agency opportunities, managing objections with finesse, and building sturdy and lasting relationships together along with your opportunities and group people. Effective conversation is the backbone of your success in community advertising and marketing and advertising and marketing, so permit's dive in and find out the secrets and techniques and strategies and techniques to becoming a keep close communicator.

The Power of Effective Communication in Network Marketing

Effective communique is the lifeblood of your community advertising and marketing and marketing and advertising and marketing business business enterprise. It allows you to supply your message simply, connect to your target audience on an emotional level, and have an effect on them to achieve this. Whether you're providing your products, sharing the enterprise possibility, or addressing objections, honing your verbal exchange talents is crucial for success.

"Communication works for people who paintings at it." - John Powell

Presenting Products or Business Opportunities

When providing your merchandise or corporation possibilities, it's miles critical to deliver a compelling and persuasive message that resonates together along with your goal market. Here are a few strategies to beautify your presentation abilties:

Know Your Audience

"Your target audience's perception is your fact." - Nancy Duarte

Understanding your audience is essential for effective conversation. Tailor your message to deal with their desires, desires, and pain factors. Speak their language, use relatable examples, and emphasize the benefits and fee your products or organisation possibility can provide.

Tell Stories that Inspire

"Stories create connection, and connection leads to movement." - Brené Brown

Stories have the energy to captivate and inspire. Use private anecdotes, fulfillment recollections, and testimonials to coloration a glittery photo of the transformational effect your merchandise or business corporation possibility can also have. Stories evoke emotions, installation credibility, and make your message memorable.

Use Visual Aids and Demonstrations

"A picture is properly genuinely worth 1000 terms." - Unknown

Visual aids and demonstrations enhance the effectiveness of your presentation. Utilize compelling visuals, product samples, or interactive demonstrations to expose off the abilities, benefits, and usage of your products. Visuals assist your target marketplace visualize the cost and impact of what you're presenting.

Example: Let's say you're imparting a fitness and well being product line. Instead of truly describing the benefits, you may show 'in advance than and after' photographs of people who have professional awesome adjustments after the use of the goods. This visual evidence offers credibility and reinforces the effectiveness of your services.

Handling Objections with Finesse

Objections are a herbal part of the earnings approach, and handling them successfully is essential for fulfillment. Here are a few strategies to cope with objections:

Listen with Empathy

"Seek first to understand, then to be understood." - Stephen R. Covey

When confronted with objections, pay interest attentively to your prospect's issues. Show empathy and renowned their angle. By without a doubt knowledge their objections, you may reply with readability and cope with their underlying dreams.

Respond with Confidence and Knowledge

"Knowledge is strength, but enthusiasm pulls the transfer." - Ivern Ball

Responding to objections requires self belief and expertise approximately your merchandise or corporation possibility. Be prepared to offer correct records, highlight relevant capabilities or advantages, and provide solutions to address your prospect's issues. Demonstrating understanding and enthusiasm can help conquer objections.

Use Testimonials and Social Proof

"Let your clients do the talking for you." - Unknown

Sharing testimonials and social proof can alleviate objections and build credibility. Provide examples of satisfied customers or a achievement organization individuals who've completed top notch effects. Testimonials create a revel in of consider and exhibit that your offerings have labored for others.

Example: Imagine a prospect raises an objection about the charge of your product. You can respond with the beneficial aid of sharing a testimonial from a client who to begin with had the same trouble however determined the product's fee some distance surpassed its price. This testimonial validates the product's virtually really worth and addresses the objection efficaciously.

Building Strong Relationships through Effective Communication

Building robust relationships is on the middle of community marketing and marketing fulfillment. Here are a few strategies to foster large connections:

Active Listening and Empathy

"Listening is the crucial component to statistics and connecting with others." - Unknown

Practice lively listening by way of giving your entire hobby in your prospects and crew individuals. Show actual hobby, ask open-ended questions, and attempting to find to recognize their needs, desires, and challenges. Empathy allows you to connect on a deeper diploma and assemble take into account.

Effective Follow-Up and Relationship Nurturing

"The fortune is within the study-up." - Jim Rohn

Follow-up is crucial for retaining relationships. Regularly attain out to your prospects and group individuals to offer aid, answer questions, and offer more assets. Personalize your interactions, take into account important info, and show actual care for their achievement.

Communicate with Authenticity and Transparency

"Honesty and transparency build remember." - Unknown

Be actual and obvious on your communication. Build consider by way of using being open about your studies, successes, or maybe worrying situations. Avoid hype or exaggerated claims, and instead, reputation on building actual connections primarily based mostly on don't forget and integrity.

"Effective communique is the cornerstone of success in network advertising and marketing. It's the bridge that connects dreams with fact." - Unknown

In this financial disaster, we explored the strength of powerful communique in community advertising and marketing. We mentioned strategies for imparting merchandise or business enterprise organisation possibilities, coping with objections with finesse, and constructing sturdy relationships through proper conversation. Remember, effective communique is a capabilities that may be advanced and diffused with exercise.

As you preserve your network advertising and marketing adventure, determine to improving your communication skills. Embrace the art work of connecting, influencing, and inspiring others thru your words and movements. By honing your verbal exchange abilties, you may assemble a strong foundation for fulfillment in network advertising and create meaningful and lasting relationships along the way.

So, skip forth, my fellow community entrepreneurs, and communicate with self assurance, empathy, and authenticity. Your phrases have the strength to convert lives and create a ripple impact of achievement within the worldwide of network advertising.

Chapter 4: Developing Leadership Skills

Nurturing Leadership Qualities and Strategies for Building and Leading a Successful Network Marketing Team

"Leadership is not about being in rate. It is set taking care of these to your charge." - Simon Sinek

Welcome to the financial ruin committed to growing control competencies in network advertising and marketing and advertising. In this bankruptcy, we are capable of delve into the critical features and techniques that make a a success community advertising and marketing leader. Leadership isn't always actually approximately managing a collection; it is approximately inspiring and empowering others to collect their entire capability. Let's find out the important thing elements of powerful manipulate and the manner you may cultivate the ones traits interior yourself and your organization.

The Role of Leadership in Network Marketing

Leadership is the inspiration of a thriving community marketing and advertising and marketing company. As a leader, your number one obligation is to create an environment that fosters growth, teamwork, and achievement. Your team appears as tons as you for steering, motivation, and manual. Embracing your manipulate feature is crucial for building a sturdy and sustainable network advertising and advertising and marketing corporation.

"Leaders turn out to be excellent, no longer due to their energy, but because of their ability to empower others." - John C. Maxwell

Nurturing Leadership Qualities

Leadership trends are not innate; they'll be advanced and nurtured. Here are a few key functions that each community advertising and marketing leader must personal:

Vision and Purpose

"A leader is one who is aware of the way, goes the way, and indicates the manner." - John C. Maxwell

A chief need to have a smooth vision and a compelling cause. Define your vision for the destiny of your group and organisation. Communicate this imaginative and prescient with passion and encourage others to rally in the again of it. Your vision have to provide a sense of direction and encourage your organization contributors to try for excellence.

Example: Imagine you have were given have been given a vision to empower human beings through the use of offering them with financial freedom via community advertising. Your reason is to help others gain their dreams and create a splendid effect on their lives. By sharing this vision together with your institution, you ignite their ardour and create a sense of cause that is going past mere financial advantage.

Self-Development and Continuous Learning

"Leadership is not a holiday spot; it's far a adventure of regular increase and self-improvement." - Robin Sharma

Great leaders are committed to their personal private increase and improvement. Continuously are attempting to find opportunities to beautify your skills, information, and attitude. Read books, attend seminars, interact in private improvement sports activities, and surround yourself with mentors and prefer-minded those who can guide your growth.

Emotional Intelligence

"Great leaders do no longer actually lead; they hook up with others on an emotional level." - Unknown

Emotional intelligence is the ability to understand and manipulate your emotions and apprehend the feelings of others. Cultivate empathy, lively listening, and powerful verbal exchange competencies. Build strong relationships based totally mostly on agree with, understand, and understanding. Emotional intelligence lets in you to connect deeply at the aspect of your team participants and create a supportive and harmonious surroundings.

Resilience and Persistence

"Leadership isn't approximately keeping off failure; it is about analyzing from failure and bouncing returned stronger." - Unknown

Leaders face traumatic situations and setbacks along their journey. It's crucial to amplify resilience and staying power. Embrace failures as opportunities for growth, examine from them, and get higher with renewed dedication. Show your organization the strength of resilience thru principal through example and upsetting them to overcome limitations.

Strategies for Building and Leading a Successful Network Marketing Team

Building a successful network advertising and advertising and marketing organization calls for powerful strategies and movements. Here are some strategies to help you foster growth and lead your group to achievement:

Lead thru Example

"Leadership isn't about being in the front; it is about being along your group." - Unknown

Be a position model in your organization individuals. Demonstrate the behaviors and movements you anticipate from them. Show strength of will, consistency, and professionalism. Lead from the the the front and inspire your team via your personal moves and effects.

Effective Communication and Collaboration

"Great leaders talk, collaborate, and create a manner of existence of cohesion and teamwork." - Unknown

Establish open and apparent verbal exchange channels internal your team. Foster a manner of existence of collaboration and teamwork. Encourage comments, listen for your group members' thoughts, and contain them in choice-making methods. Effective conversation guarantees all and sundry is aligned and operating toward commonplace goals.

Training and Support

"Great leaders do not hoard expertise; they proportion it generously with their group." - Unknown

Invest inside the training and development of your group individuals. Provide them with the essential competencies, know-how, and tools to succeed. Offer mentorship, education, and ongoing aid. By empowering your crew with the right education and help, you permit them to increase and acquire their dreams.

Recognition and Rewards

"People artwork for coins, however they go with the flow the greater mile for recognition, appreciation, and rewards." - Dale Carnegie

Acknowledge and recognize the efforts and achievements of your corporation members. Celebrate their successes, each huge and small. Recognize their hard paintings and backbone. Implement a reward gadget that motivates and incentivizes your crew to strive for excellence.

"Leadership is the paintings of empowering others to achieve greatness." - Unknown

In this economic disaster, we explored the significance of control in network advertising and advertising. We noted the traits that make an powerful chief and techniques for building and primary a a achievement network advertising and marketing and advertising and marketing agency. Remember, control is not approximately authority or manage; it's far about empowering others to unleash their entire capability and achieve superb effects.

Chapter 5: Product Knowledge and Demonstration

Deepening Knowledge and Demonstrating Value in Network Marketing

"Knowledge is electricity, mainly on the subject of community advertising." - Unknown

I welcome you to this economic catastrophe, in which we're able to discover the essential elements of product understanding and demonstration in community marketing. Your fulfillment as a network marketer carefully is primarily based completely in your capability to recognize and successfully speak the rate and advantages of the goods or services you offer. In this monetary catastrophe, we can delve into techniques to deepen your product data, amplify compelling product demonstrations, and encourage ability clients to embody the fee your services bring.

The Power of Product Knowledge

"Know your product interior out. Knowledge is contagious, and it conjures up self warranty." - Unknown

In community marketing and advertising, product information is your greatest asset. When you personal a deep knowledge of your services or products, you exude self guarantee and credibility, making it much less complicated to persuade capability clients and vendors. Let's discover a few techniques to decorate your product information:

Study the Product

Take the time to examine every difficulty of your services or products. Understand its abilities, elements, production gadget, and any precise promoting elements. The greater you recognize, the better organized you will be to deal with questions, conquer objections, and highlight the charge it offers.

Utilize Company Resources

Tap into the sources supplied by using your community marketing and marketing and advertising industrial enterprise enterprise. Attend product training periods, webinars, or conferences presented thru the organisation. Access product courses, brochures, or on-line assets that offer in-depth records approximately your offerings. Utilize those belongings to gain complete expertise approximately your products.

Use the Products Personally

To sincerely recognize and admire the price of your products, use them your self. Experience the blessings firsthand and share your private testimonials. By being a product character, you may speak authentically about the blessings and variations it may deliver.

Seek Out Testimonials

"Testimonials are the social proof that validates the effectiveness of your products." - Unknown

Collect testimonials from satisfied clients who have experienced effective effects from the usage of your products. These testimonials feature powerful social evidence and assist to collect acquire as real with among capability customers. Share those success memories to illustrate the actual-life impact of your offerings.

Creating Compelling Product Demonstrations

"A great product demonstration can speak volumes about the fee it brings." - Unknown

Once you've got were given got a sturdy understanding of your merchandise, it's time to create compelling demonstrations that captivate capability clients. Consider the following techniques:

Highlight Key Features and Benefits

Identify the unique functions and blessings of your merchandise that set them aside from others inside the market. Focus on how those features remedy precise issues or satisfy the goals of your audience. Clearly articulate the ones blessings in the direction of your demonstrations to show off the value your products provide.

Example: If you are promoting a pores and skin care product, highlight its natural components, rejuvenating houses, and potential to improve pores and skin texture and look. Emphasize how it may address unique pores and skin care troubles which consist of pimples, getting old, or dryness.

Engage the Senses

Appealing to the senses could make your product demonstration more memorable and impactful. Where possible, permit capacity customers to appearance, touch, heady scent, or even taste your products. Create an immersive experience that leaves a lasting impact.

Example: If you are promoting a fragrance, provide testers for potential customers to enjoy the heady scent firsthand. Allow them to understand its unique notes and the way it could evoke emotions and beautify their private fashion.

Address Common Concerns

"Address objections earlier than they rise up. Proactive conversation builds agree with." - Unknown

Anticipate and cope with not unusual issues or objections that functionality clients may additionally moreover have. During your demonstration, proactively offer records and rationalization to relieve any doubts they will have. By demonstrating which you recognize their issues and providing obvious answers, you assemble believe and credibility.

Example: If the price of your product is higher than similar offerings inside the market, deal with this example via manner of highlighting the advanced awesome, long-time period fee-effectiveness, or first rate substances that justify the price issue.

Tailor Demonstrations to Individuals

Every functionality patron has specific dreams and alternatives. Customize your demonstrations to align with their particular pastimes and desires. By tailoring your presentation, you're making it greater relevant and appealing to their private desires.

Example: If you are promoting a fitness supplement, recognition on one-of-a-kind elements primarily based at the man or woman's dreams. For someone interested in weight reduction, spotlight how the product can manual their adventure. For a person trying to find expanded energy, emphasize the energy and staying electricity benefits.

Inspiring Action and Follow-Up

"A compelling product demonstration with out a smooth name to motion is a ignored possibility." - Unknown

After showcasing the fee of your merchandise, it's miles vital to inspire potential clients to achieve this. Consider these strategies to set off them towards the next steps:

Clear Call to Action

Clearly speak the popular motion you want potential clients to take after the demonstration. Whether it's growing a buy, signing up as a distributor, or soliciting for more records, offer smooth instructions on how they may be capable of proceed.

Example: "To enjoy the transformative benefits of our product, in truth click on the 'Order Now' button on our internet net web page or reach out to me right away for customized help."

Follow-Up and Support

Following up with functionality clients after the demonstration is critical for constructing relationships and addressing any lingering questions or concerns. Offer custom designed useful resource and steering to assist them make an informed choice.

Example: Send a personalized electronic mail or make a phone call to check in on their thoughts about the demonstration. Address any greater questions they will have and offer similarly property or testimonials to strengthen their self perception in the goods.

In this Chapter, we explored the significance of deepening product know-how and developing compelling demonstrations in community advertising. By acquiring complete understanding approximately your merchandise, the usage of appealing demonstrations, and inspiring motion, you will be better organized to draw functionality customers and exhibit the price your offerings supply. Remember, the more you recognize and accept as genuine with on your merchandise, the extra effectively you can speak their blessings and encourage others to embody them. So, dive deep into product know-how, master the paintings of demonstration, and watch your network advertising adventure flourish.

Chapter 6: Social Media Marketing For Network Marketers

Harnessing the Power of Social Media to Expand Your Network

"Social media is not just a spoke at the wheel of advertising and marketing and marketing and advertising and marketing and advertising and marketing. It's turning into the manner whole bicycles are constructed." - Ryan Lilly

Welcome to this Chapter, in which we are able to dive into the area of social media marketing for network marketers. In this virtual age, social media structures have grow to be effective gear for growing your community, producing leads, and selling network advertising and marketing and marketing and advertising products or opportunities. This financial disaster will discover powerful techniques to make use of social media on your advantage, construct a robust non-public logo, and connect with your target market.

The Influence of Social Media in Network Marketing

"Social media lets in us to attain, interact, and impact people globally like in no way earlier than." - Unknown

Social media platforms have revolutionized the manner we be a part of and speak. They offer network marketers brilliant possibilities to extend their reap and have interaction with capacity clients and providers on a worldwide scale. Let's delve into the strategies that would enhance your social media advertising and marketing and advertising efforts:

Define Your Target Audience

To effectively appoint social media for network advertising and marketing and advertising, it's miles essential to discover and recognize your purpose market. Who are they? What are their needs, dreams, and ache elements? By defining your audience, you may tailor your content material material and messaging to resonate with their specific hobbies and motivations.

Example: If you are selling health and well-being products, your goal marketplace might likely consist of health lovers, human beings searching for herbal remedies, or those looking to decorate their everyday nicely-being.

Select the Right Platforms

Not all social media structures are created same. It's essential to choose the systems that align with your goal market and the person of your network marketing and advertising employer. Conduct studies to turn out to be privy to which systems your target audience frequents and attention your efforts there.

Example: If your intention market consists of specialists and entrepreneurs, systems like LinkedIn might be extra suitable for constructing connections and sharing business organisation-associated content.

Craft Compelling Content

"Content is fireplace, and social media is gasoline." - Jay Baer

Engaging and valuable content is the fuel that drives social media fulfillment. Create content material fabric that educates, entertains, and conjures up your target market. Share informative blog posts, fascinating movies, visually appealing pix, and idea-frightening fees that align on the facet of your community advertising and marketing organization.

Example: If you are selling a skin care logo, share pointers on pores and pores and skin care exercising routines, herbal additives, and product critiques. Showcase in advance than-and-after photos of satisfied customers to illustrate the transformative outcomes of your merchandise.

Build Relationships and Engage

"Social media isn't always about selling. It's about building relationships and which encompass cost." - Unknown

Social media is a platform for verbal exchange and connection. Engage together with your target marketplace by means of responding to feedback, starting up discussions, and addressing their inquiries. Foster a revel in of community through way of the usage of actively taking element in relevant organizations and groups.

Example: If you are selling a fitness and nutrients emblem, interact along facet your target market with the useful resource of asking questions, offering expert recommendation, and provoking them to share their health journeys. Create a supportive and interactive environment wherein they revel in valued and heard.

Building a Personal Brand

"Your personal logo is what units you apart from others. It's your particular promoting proposition." - Unknown

In network advertising and marketing and advertising, your non-public brand plays a big feature in attracting functionality customers and agencies. Let's find out strategies to assemble a compelling personal brand on social media:

Define Your Brand Identity

Determine what devices you apart from others within the network advertising industry. Identify your strengths, values, and particular tendencies that make you an actual and honest supply. Define your logo voice, aesthetics, and messaging to create a cohesive and recognizable private logo.

Example: If you are passionate about empowering people through non-public improvement, your brand would possibly reputation on motivation, self-development, and frightening fulfillment memories.

Share Your Story

"Your story is the important thing that could release someone else's prison." - Unknown

Share your adventure, reports, and successes to connect with your goal marketplace on a deeper stage. Authentic storytelling can evoke feelings and inspire others to embark on their private community advertising and marketing and advertising and marketing journeys.

Example: Share how network advertising and marketing has converted your lifestyles, whether it is economic freedom, personal boom, or the functionality to spend greater time with cherished ones. Showcasing the fine effect of community marketing through your non-public story will resonate with others who aspire for comparable achievements.

Consistency and Authenticity

Consistency is critical in building a personal logo. Maintain a everyday tone, message, and visible style for the duration of your social media structures. Be proper, transparent, and actual on your interactions and content fabric. People connect with actual tales and real human beings.

Example: If your brand emphasizes honesty, percent each your successes and disasters. Be open about the annoying conditions you have got faced and the way you have got were given conquer them. This authenticity will assemble recall and credibility together along with your goal market.

Maximizing Social Media for Network Marketing Success

"Stop being a spy, and start being a social media marketer." - Unknown

To maximize your network advertising achievement, proper here are extra techniques to encompass into your social media marketing and advertising efforts:

Utilize Social Media Advertising

Social media advertising and advertising can extensively beautify your acquire and visibility. Invest in targeted classified ads to obtain a broader goal marketplace and trap capacity clients and vendors who may not have encountered your brand in any other case.

Example: Run Facebook or Instagram classified ads targeted on particular demographics or pastimes relevant for your network advertising merchandise or opportunities.

Collaborate with Influencers

Partnering with influencers who align together together with your logo can help boom your message and reap a much broader target marketplace. Seek out influencers to your enterprise and discover collaboration possibilities which consist of product endorsements, joint campaigns, or tourist appearances on their social media systems.

Example: If you're selling a sustainable living logo, collaborate with influencers who're obsessed on green life and feature a robust following in that area of interest.

Track and Analyze Your Results

"Without records, you are surely every exceptional individual with an opinion." - W. Edwards Deming

Chapter 7: Effective Follow-Up Strategies

Nurturing Relationships and Closing Sales

"Follow-up is the key to turning possibilities into clients and clients into brand advocates."
- Unknown

Welcome to this Chapter, in which we're able to delve into the crucial topic of powerful comply with-up strategies in community marketing and marketing. Building strong relationships with possibilities and presenting properly timed and valuable data are important steps in very last income and fostering prolonged-time period patron loyalty. In this bankruptcy, we are capable of discover confirmed strategies to create a scientific follow-up method that guarantees possibilities experience supported, knowledgeable, and confident of their preference to join your network advertising and marketing commercial organisation.

The Importance of Follow-Up in Network Marketing

"Follow-up isn't always a choice; it's a determination to help your opportunities be triumphant." - Unknown

Follow-up is a important thing of the network marketing adventure. It allows you to gather acquire as proper with, deal with problems, provide additional information, and ultimately guide opportunities within the direction of creating knowledgeable alternatives. Let's delve into powerful examine-up techniques to help you nurture relationships and close to profits efficiently:

Establish a Follow-Up System

To ensure consistency and performance for your comply with-up efforts, it's miles essential to installation a systematic technique. Create a check-up gadget that outlines at the same time as and the way you'll reach out to possibilities at precise tiers of the sales technique. This gadget will assist you stay prepared and provide a unbroken enjoy for your opportunities.

Example: Use a Customer Relationship Management (CRM) device to song and manipulate your prospect interactions, set reminders for observe-up calls or emails, and display the development of each prospect.

Personalize Your Follow-Up Communications

"Personalization isn't just the usage of a person's name; it's miles about connecting with their specific desires and aspirations." - Unknown

Tailor your observe-up communications to the man or woman prospect. Reference specific conversations, address their issues, and offer data that aligns with their pursuits and desires. Personalization demonstrates your attentiveness and actual take care of their fulfillment.

Example: If a prospect expressed hobby within the bendy working hours of your community advertising and marketing and advertising opportunity, emphasize how the economic agency can in shape their desired manner of existence and highlight fulfillment memories of others who have executed work-life stability through network marketing.

Provide Value with Each Interaction

"Follow-up have to be approximately along with charge, now not just making income." - Unknown

Every comply with-up interplay want to offer some thing of fee in your possibilities. This is probably sharing informative resources, imparting beneficial suggestions or recommendation, or providing updates on applicable agency data. By usually imparting rate, you feature your self as a depended on beneficial aid and build credibility.

Example: If you are promoting health and properly-being products, share articles or movies on vitamins tips, exercise sporting events, or wholesome recipes. Offer custom designed suggestions based totally on the opportunity's unique fitness desires.

Effective Follow-Up Techniques

Now that we apprehend the importance of follow-up, permit's find out a few powerful strategies to decorate your comply with-up approach:

Timely Follow-Up

Timing is vital in take a look at-up. Reach out to opportunities promptly after initial touch or a presentation to capitalize on their interest and preserve momentum. Delayed observe-up can also bring about overlooked possibilities or a lack of interest.

Example: Within 24-forty eight hours of a prospect attending a presentation, deliver a customized observe-up electronic mail thanking them for their time and summarizing key elements mentioned. Offer to address any questions or issues they may have.

Variety of Communication Channels

Diversify your comply with-up strategies via utilizing numerous communique channels. While cellular phone calls and emails are commonplace, remember leveraging precise structures which incorporates social media messaging or video calls to have interaction opportunities in outstanding approaches and cater to their options.

Example: If a prospect is energetic on social media, connect to them thru structures like Facebook Messenger or LinkedIn to offer updates, answer questions, and proportion precious content cloth.

Active Listening and Responding

"Listen with the motive to understand, not just to reply." - Unknown

During observe-up conversations, practice lively listening. Give your opportunities suitable enough opportunity to proportion their mind, issues, and questions. Respond without a doubt, demonstrating empathy and addressing their precise desires and hobbies.

Example: If a prospect expresses concerns approximately the initial funding required, pay interest attentively, and offer specific facts on the functionality return on funding, achievement recollections, and the help gadget to be had to help them be successful.

Closing the Sale Through Follow-Up

Effective examine-up plays a big characteristic in remaining earnings and welcoming possibilities to sign up for your community advertising and advertising business organisation. Here are a few strategies to guide potentialities towards a brilliant selection:

Recap and Reiterate Benefits

Revisit the key blessings and advantages of your network marketing and advertising and advertising possibility or products all through comply with-up conversations. Remind potentialities of the rate they stand to advantage and the manner it aligns with their dreams and aspirations.

Example: Summarize the monetary ability, bendy manner of life, private improvement possibilities, and the supportive community that comes with turning into a member of your community advertising and marketing business enterprise.

Address Objections and Concerns

Anticipate objections and issues that possibilities may additionally beautify and be prepared with nicely-crafted responses. Address their fears or doubts straight away and provide helping proof, testimonials, or success recollections to relieve their worries.

Example: If a prospect is hesitant about community advertising's legitimacy, share splendid company information, testimonials from a success network entrepreneurs, and your very own personal opinions to construct receive as authentic with and credibility.

Create a Sense of Urgency

Encourage possibilities to take action with the resource of developing a enjoy of urgency. Highlight restrained-time gives, specific bonuses, or incentives available for those who be part of or make a purchase inner a specific time-body.

Chapter 8: Team Building and Duplication

Unleashing the Power of Collaboration and Replication

"Teamwork makes the dream work." - John C. Maxwell

Welcome to this Chapter, where we're capable of delve into the critical project rely of organization building and duplication in community advertising and marketing and advertising and advertising. Building a robust and triggered team is critical for prolonged-term achievement in this commercial enterprise agency. By fostering a tradition of collaboration and implementing effective duplication strategies, you can growth your efforts and create exponential increase interior your organisation. In this bankruptcy, we will discover established strategies and strategies to build a thriving group and mirror fulfillment.

The Power of Team Building in Network Marketing

"Alone we're capable of accomplish that little; together we will collect this a exquisite deal." - Helen Keller

Network marketing and advertising and advertising and marketing and marketing isn't always a solo undertaking. It prospers on the power of teamwork. Let's dive into the crucial element additives of crew constructing to help you create a encouraged and high-performing group:

Establish a Vision and Shared Goals

A sturdy employer is united via a commonplace imaginative and prescient and shared goals. Clearly articulate your community advertising and marketing and advertising vision and outline viable desires that align with the aspirations of your group participants. When anybody is running inside the route of a common reason, collaboration and synergy are heightened.

Example: "Our vision is to empower humans to obtain economic freedom and private boom thru our community marketing commercial corporation. Our shared intention is to help a hundred people earn a six-determine income within the subsequent one year."

Foster a Culture of Collaboration and Support

Encourage collaboration and create an environment wherein organization individuals experience valued and supported. Foster open conversation channels, offer mentorship and education opportunities, and understand and feature fun the achievements of organization contributors. A lifestyle of collaboration builds accept as true with and complements group harmony.

Example: Conduct regular group conferences, brainstorming intervals, and education workshops to inspire idea sharing, skills development, and mutual manual.

Lead through Example

As a pacesetter, it's far vital to manual via instance. Demonstrate the functions and behaviors you expect from your organization members. Show electricity of will, resilience, integrity, and a sturdy paintings ethic. Your movements will encourage and encourage your institution to comply with healthy.

Example: Be the primary to reap and the closing to move away at crew sports activities. Show enthusiasm, take initiative, and usually work closer to your desires.

Duplication: Replicating Success Within Your Organization

Duplication is the critical component to sustainable growth in network advertising and marketing. It consists of coaching your group members to replicate your achievement by means of the use of manner of following a proven device. Let's discover effective duplication strategies:

Simplify and Systemize

Create a easy and duplicatable device that your group contributors can with out issues have a examine. Break down the machine of constructing the business into actionable steps, offering easy pointers and assets. A simplified machine will boom the probabilities of a fulfillment replication.

Example: Develop step-via the usage of-step training substances, scripts, and templates that define the prospecting, presentation, and have a observe-up strategies. Provide results to be had training movies or modules that guide business enterprise people thru every level.

Mentorship and Training

Effective mentorship and education are vital for duplication. Offer ongoing help, schooling, and education for your team individuals, ensuring they've got the critical skills and recognize-the manner to mirror your success. Empower them to become leaders themselves.

Example: Conduct everyday schooling instructions on diverse components of network advertising, which includes prospecting, effective verbal exchange, and manage improvement. Provide one-on-one training to address character traumatic situations and provide customized steerage.

Encourage and Recognize Achievements

Acknowledging and celebrating the achievements of your group members fosters a way of life of motivation and achievement. Recognize milestones, rank advancements, and incredible performances. This not best boosts morale however additionally evokes others to attempt for his or her very very personal successes.

Example: Highlight institution humans' accomplishments in the direction of institution conferences, on social media systems, or in newsletters. Offer incentives and rewards for achieving unique objectives.

Chapter 9: Time Management And Productivity

Unlocking Your Full Potential in Network Marketing

"Time is what we want maximum, but what we use worst." - William Penn

Welcome to this Chapter, in which we are able to discover the crucial hassle count of time control and productiveness inside the context of network advertising and advertising and marketing. Time is a valuable aid, and coping with it correctly is crucial for accomplishing achievement for your network advertising and advertising industrial company. In this financial disaster, we're able to delve into tested techniques and techniques that will help you prioritize obligations, maximize productiveness, and make the most of your to be had time.

Understanding the Importance of Time Management

"Success isn't always pretty much making the right picks; it is also about coping with some time efficiently." - Unknown

Effective time manipulate is the foundation of productivity and success in network marketing and advertising and marketing. Let's have a examine why time manage is essential:

Setting Clear Goals and Priorities

Time control lets in you to set clean dreams and priorities. By defining your goals and aligning them along with your community marketing and advertising and marketing business organisation, you may cognizance some time and energy on responsibilities that make contributions to your prolonged-term achievement.

Example: Prioritize earnings-producing sports activities which include prospecting, observe-ups, and group constructing over less critical tasks like checking emails or surfing social media.

Maximizing Productivity and Efficiency

Proper time manage permits you to maximise productivity and overall performance. By allocating a while successfully, you can accomplish more in lots an awful lot less time, leaving room for private increase and a balanced life.

Example: Use time-blockading techniques to allocate specific time slots for tremendous activities, including prospecting inside the morning, schooling in the afternoon, and personal improvement within the midnight.

Reducing Stress and Overwhelm

Effective time manipulate reduces pressure and overwhelm. By organizing your responsibilities, placing realistic final dates, and growing a structured time desk, you can approach your paintings with a smooth mind and a experience of manage.

Example: Break down huge responsibilities or desires into smaller, plausible duties.

Prioritize them based on urgency and importance to avoid feeling beaten.

Techniques for Effective Time Management in Network Marketing

"Now is the handiest time you've got got were given. Make the maximum of it." - Robert Kiyosaki

Now, allow's discover practical strategies and techniques for coping with some time efficaciously in network advertising:

Prioritize Your Tasks

Identify your maximum vital responsibilities and prioritize them based totally on their impact in your community advertising and marketing agency. Focus on excessive-fee sports that align collectively with your desires and generate the maximum full-size consequences.

Example: Make a every day to-do list, highlighting the top three duties that need to be completed to move your commercial company ahead.

Time Blocking

Time blocking is a effective approach that involves scheduling specific blocks of time for one-of-a-type sports. Dedicate uninterrupted periods for vital responsibilities and avoid distractions within the route of those time slots.

Example: Reserve a block of time inside the morning for prospecting and a separate block within the afternoon for group schooling or private improvement.

Delegate and Outsource

Recognize tasks that may be delegated or outsourced to others, together with administrative work or image format. Focus your power on sports that leverage your strengths and expertise.

Example: Hire a virtual assistant to address recurring administrative obligations, freeing up it gradual to interest on earnings-generating sports activities.

Eliminate Time Wasters

Identify and do away with sports activities that devour some time without which include cost on your community advertising and marketing and advertising and marketing and advertising and marketing employer. Minimize distractions, which encompass immoderate social media use or immoderate time spent on non-commercial enterprise-associated obligations.

Example: Set specific very last dates for social media utilization and use productiveness system to dam distracting internet web sites or apps at some point of different paintings hours.

Continual Learning and Personal Development

Invest time in non-stop studying and personal development to enhance your talents and stay up to date with enterprise developments.

This funding pays off in the end thru developing your general performance and effectiveness.

Example: Dedicate part of your day or week to studying books, attending webinars, or being attentive to podcasts that focus on private growth and community advertising strategies.

In this Chapter, we explored the essential characteristic of time manage and productivity in network advertising. By understanding the importance of effective time control, putting clean goals, maximizing productiveness, and implementing realistic strategies, you can launch your entire ability on your network advertising and marketing business agency. Remember, time is a precious beneficial beneficial resource, and how you manipulate it'll at once impact your achievement.

Chapter 10: Overcoming Objections and Rejections

Turning Challenges into Opportunities in Network Marketing

"The largest limitations in life are the limits our thoughts creates." - Unknown

Welcome to this bankruptcy, in which we're able to discover the art of overcoming objections and rejections in community advertising. Objections and rejections are inevitable in any earnings-based business agency, but they can be transformed into opportunities for increase and fulfillment. In this financial ruin, we're able to delve into effective strategies and techniques to address not unusual objections and rejections confronted in community advertising and marketing and advertising.

Understanding Objections and Rejections in Network Marketing

"Objections are not roadblocks; they're stepping stones toward achievement." - Unknown

Objections and rejections are part of the network advertising and marketing journey. They may additionally moreover stand up due to numerous motives along with skepticism, lack of know-how, or non-public situations. Understanding the nature of objections and rejections is crucial for effectively addressing them:

Common Objections in Network Marketing

Common objections in community advertising and marketing embody troubles about the legitimacy of the economic enterprise version, skepticism about the goods or services, fear of failure or economic risks, and poor beyond critiques. Each objection affords an possibility to educate, make clear, and construct accept as true with.

Example: When a person will increase the objection of "Is this a pyramid scheme?" you may provide an reason behind the jail and moral shape of community marketing and advertising, highlighting the focus on product earnings and the functionality for person fulfillment.

Dealing with Rejections

Rejections are part of the adventure and need to not be taken for my part. They regularly stem from factors past your control, which includes timing, private opportunities, or man or woman situations. Learning how to attend to rejections gracefully and professionally is essential to retaining relationships and turning them into destiny possibilities.

Example: Instead of feeling discouraged with the aid of way of a rejection, hobby on retaining a brilliant relationship with the opportunity. Stay connected and comply with up periodically, as situations and interests might also moreover trade over time.

Strategies for Overcoming Objections and Rejections

"To triumph over objections, you need to recognize them, empathize with them, and respond with self belief." - Unknown

Now, allow's discover effective strategies for overcoming objections and rejections in community advertising and marketing and marketing:

Active Listening and Empathy

Listen attentively to the chance's objections, empathize with their issues, and trying to find to understand their thoughts-set. This approach builds agree with and permits you to address their unique troubles correctly.

Example: Repeat the objection lower back to the opportunity, displaying which you recognize their element of view. Respond with empathy, acknowledging their issues and providing reassurance or more data to cope with them.

Educate and Provide Information

Address objections with the useful resource of providing accurate and relevant statistics approximately your network advertising and marketing agency, products, or reimbursement plan. Educating possibilities facilitates to dispel misconceptions and collect credibility.

Example: Share success memories of people who have done fantastic consequences to your community advertising and marketing commercial enterprise. Provide testimonials, case research, or product records that highlights the charge and advantages.

Share Your Personal Story

Personal stories create connection and encourage take transport of as right with. Share your personal opinions and journey in network advertising and advertising and marketing, emphasizing the manner you overcame objections and grew to come to be rejections into stepping stones in the course of fulfillment.

Example: Share a private tale of the way you to begin with had doubts or faced rejections however continued, determined out from the opinions, and subsequently carried out big success. This narrative display off resilience and encourages possibilities to appearance objections as opportunities for increase.

Offer Solutions and Benefits

Highlight the answers and benefits that your network marketing enterprise or merchandise can provide to deal with the danger's issues. Focus on how your company can enhance their lives, satisfy their goals, or meet their precise dreams.

Example: If a prospect is involved approximately economic dangers, emphasize the low startup expenses, flexible earning ability, and the help tool supplied through your network advertising industrial agency enterprise enterprise.

Follow-Up and Relationship Building

Maintaining relationships and regular comply with-up are vital in overcoming objections and rejections. Stay associated with possibilities, offer greater records as needed, and maintain constructing rapport through the years.

Example: Keep a record of objections and rejections encountered and follow up with possibilities periodically. Share valuable content material cloth, fulfillment memories, or updates about your network advertising and advertising and marketing organisation to maintain them engaged and informed.

Chapter 11: Personal Branding and Online Presence

Unleashing Your Network Marketing Potential

"Your private logo is what human beings say approximately you even as you're now not within the room." - Jeff Bezos

Welcome to this bankruptcy, wherein we're capable of dive into the power of private branding and on line presence in network advertising. Building a strong non-public logo and setting up a compelling online presence are vital for fulfillment in cutting-edge virtual age. In this bankruptcy, we're capable of discover effective strategies and techniques to craft your private logo, set up credibility, and leverage on line systems for enterprise increase.

Understanding Personal Branding in Network Marketing

"Your brand is a story unfolding throughout all client touchpoints." - Jonah Sachs

Defining Your Personal Brand

Your non-public logo is the unique mixture of your skills, values, personality, and reviews that set you other than others inside the community advertising and marketing industry. It is the way you present yourself to the arena and the way others apprehend you. Defining your personal logo is the inspiration for building trust, credibility, and effect.

Example: Reflect on your strengths, passions, and values. Identify what makes you specific and the manner you could align that on the aspect of your network marketing business. Develop a smooth emblem message that resonates with your target marketplace.

Establishing Credibility and Trust

Credibility is important in network marketing. Building take transport of as right with together along with your goal market is vital for attracting and preserving customers and institution individuals. Establishing your self as an professional and a dependable deliver of information will support your private brand.

Example: Share valuable content material material, insights, and data thru blog posts, social media, or films. Provide answers to common disturbing situations confronted thru the usage of your target market. Consistency and authenticity are key to building credibility.

Leveraging Online Platforms for Personal Branding

"Your on-line presence is your global storefront." - Dharmesh Shah

Creating a Professional Website or Blog

A properly-designed net web website or weblog serves as your online hub, showcasing your non-public logo and supplying a platform to percentage precious content material fabric, have interaction along with your audience, and seize leads.

Example: Create a internet site or weblog that displays your personal logo. Include an approximately page to introduce your self, a weblog to percentage your information, and a hint internet net page for inquiries and collaboration possibilities.

Building a Strong Social Media Presence

Social media systems offer incredible opportunities to hook up with a bigger target audience, assemble relationships, and increase your non-public emblem. Choose systems in which your target market is maximum energetic and engage continuously.

Example: Develop a social media approach that aligns collectively together along with your non-public brand. Share valuable content material, have interaction with your goal market, and take part in relevant employer conversations. Be genuine and aware about construct authentic connections.

Harnessing the Power of Video Marketing

Video content cloth has turn out to be more and more well-known in current years. Utilize structures like YouTube, Facebook Live, or Instagram Stories to create enticing motion pictures that exhibit your data, percent testimonials, or provide valuable suggestions.

Example: Record video tutorials, product demonstrations, or testimonials to set up your self as an expert to your community advertising and advertising and marketing and advertising and advertising and marketing place of interest. Engage along aspect your target market by way of website hosting live Q&A intervals or interviews with company experts.

Engaging in Influencer Marketing

Collaborating with influencers or idea leaders within the network advertising and marketing and advertising business enterprise can extend your obtain and beautify your personal brand. Identify influencers whose values align with yours and discover collaboration opportunities.

Example: Partner with influencers for joint webinars, tourist weblog posts, or social media takeovers. This lets in you to faucet into their goal marketplace and leverage their credibility to decorate your private emblem.

Nurturing and Evolving Your Personal Brand

"Your non-public logo is a non-forestall artwork in development." - Tom Peters

Consistency and Authenticity

Consistency and authenticity are the pillars of a strong personal emblem. Continuously supply value, live right to your values, and interact along with your goal market in an actual and significant manner.

Example: Maintain a constant emblem voice all through all your on-line systems. Be proper and apparent to your interactions. Your target audience will appreciate your authenticity and trustworthiness.

Monitoring and Adapting

Monitor your on-line presence and adapt your non-public emblem approach as wanted. Stay updated with the current-day dispositions and techniques in personal branding to stay relevant and resonate together at the side of your target marketplace.

Example: Regularly assessment your on line profiles, internet internet website, and content cloth material. Analyze target market engagement, remarks, and market developments. Make essential changes to make certain your personal emblem evolves with the changing landscape.

In the sector of network advertising and marketing, non-public branding and on-line presence are powerful system to differentiate yourself from the opposition and attraction to the right aim marketplace. By defining your non-public logo, establishing credibility, and leveraging on line structures, you may unharness your community advertising and marketing and advertising potential and create lasting connections with customers and institution people. Remember, constructing a non-public brand is an ongoing method that requires consistency, authenticity, and flexibility. Embrace the adventure, show off your unique price, and allow your non-public logo shine inside the virtual realm of community advertising and advertising and marketing and advertising.

Chapter 12: Financial Management and Goal Setting

Unlocking Your Network Marketing Success

"Setting goals is the first step in turning the invisible into the scene." - Tony Robbins

Welcomes to this bankruptcy, wherein we're capable of delve into the critical elements of monetary control and motive installing community advertising and marketing. Understanding the income ability, developing a economic plan, and putting sensible profits dreams are crucial for building a sustainable and worthwhile community marketing and advertising industrial agency. In this bankruptcy, we are capable of discover techniques and techniques to empower you with monetary literacy and manual you in putting conceivable profits desires.

Understanding the Income Potential in Network Marketing

"Network advertising and marketing is the huge wave of the destiny. It's taking the area of franchising, which now calls for an excessive amount of capital for the average man or woman." - Jim Rohn

Embracing the Network Marketing Opportunity

Network advertising and marketing gives a completely specific income capability that permits human beings to assemble their non-public organizations with out the conventional overhead prices. Understanding the earning opportunities in network advertising is critical for putting sensible profits dreams.

Example: Research achievement stories and earnings evaluations of a achievement network marketers to your agency. This will provide you with insights into the income potential and encourage you to strive for similar fulfillment.

Leveraging Compensation Plans

Each community advertising and marketing and advertising and marketing corporation has its non-public compensation plan that outlines how vendors are rewarded for their efforts. Familiarize yourself on the facet of your organisation's repayment plan to understand the severa earnings streams and incentives available to you.

Example: Study the compensation plan and grow to be aware of the wonderful strategies you may earn income, collectively with retail profits, crew commissions, bonuses, or incentives. This information will help you maximize your earning functionality.

Creating a Financial Plan

"By failing to prepare, you are on the brink of fail." - Benjamin Franklin

Tracking Income and Expenses

To manipulate your price range efficiently, start by using the use of using monitoring your income and costs. This will provide you with a clean photograph of your economic state of affairs and help you are making informed picks about budgeting and making an funding.

Example: Keep an in depth file of your network marketing and advertising and marketing and advertising income, in addition to any agency-related costs. Utilize budgeting equipment or software program software to tune and categorize your earnings and prices for better monetary manipulate.

Budgeting and Saving

Creating a price range is critical for allocating your profits because it have to be and ensuring you have sufficient finances for every personal and organisation goals. Incorporate monetary monetary savings into your fee range to assemble a monetary safety internet and invest in your community advertising and marketing corporation.

Example: Set unique charge variety classes in your private and organization prices. Allocate a part of your earnings toward economic financial savings and investment opportunities to gas the increase of your network advertising and marketing and marketing company.

Setting Realistic Income Goals

"Goals are goals with last dates." - Diana Scharf

Setting S.M.A.R.T. Goals

Setting realistic income goals is crucial for staying prompted and focused for your community marketing adventure. Use the S.M.A.R.T. Purpose-setting framework to ensure your desires are Specific, Measurable, Achievable, Relevant, and Time-certain.

Example: Instead of placing a indistinct purpose like "incomes extra money," set a particular income goal for a specific duration. For example, "I will earn $five,000 in month-to-month commissions in the subsequent three hundred and sixty five days."

Breaking Down Goals into Actionable Steps

Once you've got set your earnings goals, break them down into smaller, actionable steps. This will make your goals more feasible and could let you music your development efficiently.

Example: Identify the sports and milestones a very good way to make a contribution to your income purpose. For instance, developing your customer base, recruiting new team participants, or conducting particular income goals. Set final dates for every milestone to maintain yourself accountable.

Achieving Financial Success in Network Marketing

"It's not approximately the cash. It's about the liberty." - Robert Kiyosaki

Continuous Learning and Skill Development

Invest in your private and expert growth through the usage of constantly studying and developing the abilties important for economic success in network advertising. Enhance your know-how of income, advertising and advertising and marketing, management, and financial control.

Example: Attend organisation conferences, look at books on network advertising and advertising and marketing and monetary control, and participate in training applications or webinars to enlarge your information and capability set.

Mentorship and Collaboration

Surround your self with a hit community entrepreneurs and are in search of mentorship from the ones who have executed economic fulfillment. Collaborate with like-minded people who percentage your dreams and aspirations.

Chapter 13: Compliance and Ethical Practices

Building a Strong Foundation for Network Marketing Success

"Success without integrity is failure in cover." - Unknown

Welcome to this financial catastrophe, in which we can find out the essential importance of compliance and moral practices within the network advertising industry. It is critical for network entrepreneurs to recognize and abide thru enterprise recommendations, hold moral necessities, and ensure compliance with prison necessities. In this financial wreck, we are capable of delve into the vital thing factors of compliance and ethical practices and provide you with the facts and device to construct a sturdy basis for your network advertising success.

Understanding Industry Regulations

"Compliance with jail tips and pointers isn't always a burden. It's a fee proposition." - Sheryl Sandberg

Educating Yourself on Industry Regulations

To make certain compliance and ethical practices, network entrepreneurs should have a easy information of the criminal tips and suggestions that govern the company. This understanding will help you use inside the barriers and defend your business employer and reputation.

Example: Familiarize your self with the pointers installation via using applicable governing our bodies, which embody the Federal Trade Commission (FTC), Direct Selling Association (DSA), and community regulatory agencies. Stay updated on any changes or updates to those rules.

Know Your Company's Policies and Procedures

Each network marketing enterprise enterprise has its very personal set of rules and methods that govern the behavior of its groups. It is essential to familiarize yourself with those tips and make certain compliance to hold a professional and ethical commercial company exercise.

Example: Carefully evaluate your company's guidelines and strategies manual. Understand the guidelines for product claims, profits representations, recruiting practices, and customer service. Adhere to the ones regulations to protect your business and hold a effective reputation.

Upholding Ethical Standards

"Ethics is understanding the distinction among what you have the right to do and what is the proper component to do." - Potter Stewart

Transparency and Honesty

Ethical community marketers prioritize transparency and honesty in their interactions with potentialities, customers, and institution people. Building accept as genuine with thru sincere conversation is vital for prolonged-term achievement within the corporation.

Example: Always offer correct and honest data approximately your products, compensation plan, and employer opportunity. Avoid making fake claims or misrepresenting the potential results of turning into a member of your network marketing enterprise.

Respecting Privacy and Consent

Respecting the privacy and consent of individuals is a essential moral principle. Network marketers want to attain proper consent in advance than contacting possibilities or sharing their personal facts with zero.33 events.

Example: Seek permission earlier than which includes people in your touch listing or sending them promotional substances. Respect their choice within the occasion that they select out out not to take part or preference to unsubscribe from your communications.

Ensuring Compliance with Legal Requirements

"Ethics and compliance are not the same aspect, but they will be inseparable." - Michael Volkov

Tax and Legal Obligations

Network entrepreneurs want to satisfy their tax and crook obligations to perform their groups ethically and responsibly. Familiarize yourself with the tax criminal pointers and guidelines relevant for your community marketing organisation and speak over with experts, if wished.

Example: Keep correct data of your organization charges, profits, and taxes. Consult with a tax professional to make certain compliance with close by tax legal guidelines and tips unique to community advertising and advertising and advertising.

Consumer Protection and Anti-Pyramid Scheme Laws

To maintain a high excellent recognition for the organization, it's miles crucial to recognize and comply with purchaser safety crook recommendations and tips. Avoid carrying out sports activities that may be perceived as pyramid schemes or illegal enterprise agency practices.

Example: Educate yourself about the characteristics that differentiate valid community advertising organizations from pyramid schemes. Ensure that your industrial agency practices align with the necessities and tips set with the aid of regulatory authorities.

Chapter 14: Personal Development and Continuous Learning

Unlocking Your Potential within the Network Marketing Industry

"Invest in yourself. Your career is the engine of your wealth." - Paul Clitheroe

Welcome to Chapter 15, in which we discover the essential feature of private improvement and non-forestall mastering within the dynamic global of community advertising and marketing and advertising. In this financial ruin, we are able to delve into the significance of personal growth, self-development, and non-prevent gaining knowledge of to stay in advance and thrive inside the ever-evolving community advertising and advertising and advertising industry. By embracing private development and committing to lifelong mastering, you can release your complete capacity and benefit exquisite fulfillment for your community advertising and advertising and marketing adventure.

The Power of Personal Development

"Personal improvement is a top time-saver. The higher you come to be, the loads much less time it takes you to benefit your dreams." - Brian Tracy

Cultivating a Growth Mindset

Personal development starts offevolved with cultivating a boom mind-set—a belief that your capabilities and competencies can be superior via willpower and tough artwork. By adopting a growth mind-set, you open yourself as lots as new opportunities and come to be proactive in attempting to find personal and expert increase.

Example: Embrace worrying conditions, view setbacks as possibilities for mastering and development, and are seeking out remarks from mentors and peers to continuously make bigger your talents and competencies.

Self-Reflection and Self-Awareness

Self-mirrored photograph and self-interest are important for non-public improvement. By taking the time to understand yourself, your strengths, weaknesses, and regions for improvement, you could embark on a adventure of self-improvement and personal boom.

Example: Set apart regular time for self-mirrored image. Assess your actions, behaviors, and mind-set. Identify regions wherein you excel and regions wherein you may similarly amplify. Use this expertise to create a roadmap for your private boom.

Continuous Learning for Success

"Formal schooling will make you a living; self-education will make you a fortune." - Jim Rohn

Embracing a Learning Mindset

In the short-paced worldwide of community advertising and marketing, non-forestall reading is critical to stay earlier of the curve. Embrace a studying mind-set that prioritizes acquiring new expertise, skills, and insights to gasoline your achievement.

Example: Make studying a each day addiction. Read books, pay attention to podcasts, attend seminars, and interact in on line courses that decorate your information of network advertising and marketing and advertising and marketing and advertising strategies, personal improvement, management, and outstanding applicable subjects.

Networking and Learning from Others

Network advertising and marketing and marketing affords a completely precise opportunity to connect to a success individuals who can function mentors and function fashions. Leverage those connections to study from their reviews and benefit precious insights.

Example: Attend business agency occasions, be part of mastermind corporations, and actively interact with a success network entrepreneurs. Seek recommendation, ask questions, and have a look at from their trips to enhance up your personal private and expert boom.

Personal Growth Strategies in Network Marketing

"The great investment you could make is in yourself." - Warren Buffett

Goal Setting and Planning

Set clean, actionable goals and develop a plan to acquire them. Goal putting gives hobby, motivation, and a roadmap on your personal improvement journey.

Example: Define particular, measurable, manageable, relevant, and time-high-quality (SMART) dreams for one-of-a-type elements of your community advertising and marketing and marketing commercial agency and private life. Break them down into actionable steps and display your progress frequently.

Building Resilience and Overcoming Challenges

The network advertising adventure isn't always with out its stressful conditions. Building resilience and growing the ability to get higher from setbacks are critical for personal boom and success inside the corporation.

Example: Cultivate resilience through reframing setbacks as possibilities for analyzing and growth. Develop coping strategies, are trying to find manual from mentors and friends, and hold a powerful attitude even in hard instances.

Self-Care and Work-Life Balance

Taking care of yourself is vital for lengthy-term fulfillment in community advertising and advertising and advertising and marketing. Prioritize self-care, preserve a wholesome art work-lifestyles balance, and nurture your not unusual nicely-being.

Example: Set boundaries, workout self-care sports which incorporates exercising, meditation, and spending best time with loved ones. Create a time table that lets in for committed time for work, personal increase, and rest.

In this bankruptcy, we explored the significance of personal development and non-save you getting to know in the community advertising and marketing and marketing industry. By making an funding to your private boom, embracing a studying mind-set, and imposing effective personal growth strategies, you function yourself for prolonged-time period fulfillment. Remember, non-public development is a adventure, and non-save you reading is a lifelong pursuit. Commit to your boom, include exchange, and unharness your whole ability inside the dynamic international of network advertising.

Chapter 15: Cultivate a Splendid Mindset

In the sector of network advertising and advertising and marketing, cultivating a superb thoughts-set and maintaining a strong belief for your abilities are important factors which can drastically impact your achievement. A fantastic mind-set permits you to conquer stressful situations, live caused, and method your community marketing commercial corporation with enthusiasm. This summary explores the significance of cultivating a tremendous attitude and offers realistic techniques to help you make bigger and keep it at some point of your journey.

Recognize the Power of a Positive Mindset

A powerful mind-set serves as the muse for success in community marketing. It allows you to preserve optimism, navigate limitations, and persevere within the face of setbacks. By recognizing the electricity of a high-quality attitude, you may harness its advantages and create a thriving network advertising and advertising and marketing and advertising enterprise.

Embrace Self-Belief and Confidence

Believing in yourself and your abilties is important for fulfillment. Develop a strong feel of self-perception via acknowledging your strengths, celebrating your achievements, and reframing any self-doubts into opportunities for boom. Cultivate self perception through non-forestall analyzing, searching out statistics, and growing information to your area.

Practice Self-Care and Personal Development

To maintain a nice mind-set, it is important to prioritize self-care and private improvement. Take care of your physical and intellectual nicely-being via the use of carrying out activities that nourish your frame and thoughts. This includes exercising, meditation, pursuing interests, and on the lookout for private growth through studying, attending workshops, or carrying out reflective practices.

Surround Yourself with Positivity

The organization you hold appreciably impacts your mind-set. Surround yourself with excessive nice, like-minded folks who aid and uplift you. Seek out mentors, be a part of community advertising and marketing groups, and engage in mastermind businesses in which you could examine from a achievement human beings within the employer. By immersing your self in a pleasant surroundings, you can fuel your private positivity and motivation.

Practice Gratitude and Visualization

Gratitude and visualization strategies are effective tools for cultivating a incredible thoughts-set. Practice gratitude each day with the useful aid of acknowledging and appreciating the benefits for your existence, every large and small. Visualize your goals and goals as though they have got already been completed, allowing yourself to experience the emotions and pleasure related to your fulfillment. This exercising permits help a fantastic outlook and keeps you focused for your aspirations.

Reframe Challenges as Opportunities

In network advertising and advertising and marketing, traumatic situations are inevitable. However, by way of manner of reframing traumatic conditions as opportunities for growth and gaining knowledge of, you can maintain a effective attitude even within the course of tough times. Embrace setbacks as valuable education, adapt your techniques, and approach obstacles with a trouble-fixing mind-set. Viewing stressful conditions as stepping stones in vicinity of roadblocks will assist you to persevere and hold moving ahead.

Monitor and Reframe Negative Thoughts

Negative mind can keep away from your improvement and hose down your mindset.

Pay hobby to your inner speak and emerge as aware of any ordinary awful mind or self-restricting beliefs. Challenge and reframe those mind via changing them with effective affirmations and empowering statements. Regularly confirm your competencies, capacity, and the great impact you could make via your community advertising and advertising enterprise business enterprise.

Celebrate Small Wins

Acknowledging and celebrating your achievements, regardless of how small, is critical for keeping a nice mindset. Celebrate your improvement, milestones, and successes alongside the manner. By recognizing your accomplishments, you enhance a high-quality outlook and raise your motivation to maintain striving for extra large achievements.

Conclusion

Cultivating a extraordinary mind-set and maintaining a sturdy belief on your abilties are important additives of a a fulfillment network marketing and advertising and marketing journey. By embracing self-notion, working towards self-care, surrounding your self with positivity, and reframing demanding situations, you can foster a nice thoughts-set that fuels your fulfillment. Remember, your attitude is internal your manipulate, and thru nurturing it, you empower your self to overcome barriers, embody opportunities, and assemble a thriving network

Set clear and conceivable dreams to guide your efforts

In the area of community advertising, setting clean and practicable dreams is a fundamental difficulty of achievement. Goals function guiding beacons, presenting course and reputation on your efforts. This precis explores the significance of placing goals and gives practical techniques that will help you set up easy and conceivable goals in an effort to strain your community advertising and marketing journey forward.

The Significance of Goal Setting

Setting dreams in community advertising and advertising is critical for severa motives. Goals provide clarity and cause, supporting you prioritize your sports and allocate assets effectively. They function benchmarks for measuring development and success, permitting you to track your achievements and make critical modifications along the way. By putting easy and workable desires, you may decorate your motivation, maintain consciousness, and create a roadmap toward the consciousness of your aspirations.

Start with a Vision

Before setting unique desires, it's miles crucial to installation a compelling vision in your network advertising agency. Your imaginative and prescient represents the last excursion spot you need to attain and serves as the inspiration to your goals. Visualize the destiny you choice, considering elements which includes monetary freedom, private boom, impact on others, and the lifestyle you reason to gain. By clarifying your imaginative and prescient, you may align your goals along with your overarching motive and create a revel in of passion and resolution.

SMART Goals

The SMART framework offers a based approach to aim putting. SMART stands for Specific, Measurable, Achievable, Relevant, and Time-sure. Specific desires really outline what you want to acquire, which encompass a particular rank or earnings aim. Measurable dreams allow you to song improvement objectively, frequently via quantifiable metrics. Achievable desires are sensible and internal your collect, thinking about your modern assets and talents. Relevant desires align together with your normal vision and values. Finally, time-certain desires have a selected cut-off date or time frame, making sure a experience of urgency and obligation.

Break Goals into Milestones

Breaking your desires into smaller milestones allows create a experience of progress and success. By dividing your overarching goals into manageable duties or sub-desires, you could have a good time milestones alongside the manner, keeping motivation and momentum. These milestones act as stepping stones in the route of your huge dreams and allow you to look into your development, make critical adjustments, and live on route.

Prioritize and Focus

In network marketing, it's miles crucial to prioritize your goals and consciousness your efforts on the maximum impactful sports activities. Determine which goals are maximum aligned together with your vision and have the capability to yield giant consequences. Prioritization allows you keep away from spreading yourself too skinny and allows you to channel your power and assets in the direction of the maximum essential goals. Focus at the obligations and strategies for you to have the maximum widespread effect for your corporation boom and achievement.

Create an Action Plan

An movement plan outlines the particular steps and techniques you will undertake to acquire your dreams. Break down every aim into actionable responsibilities and create a roadmap that outlines the gathering, timeline, and assets required for every step. Your movement plan will feature a practical manual, supplying clarity and form to your each day activities. Regularly examine and modify your action plan as essential, making sure it remains aligned along with your evolving business wishes.

Track and Measure Progress

Regularly monitoring and measuring your development is crucial for staying on direction and making informed alternatives. Establish key regularly occurring normal overall performance signs (KPIs) or metrics that assist you to objectively look into your development in the route of each intention. Utilize gear, which include spreadsheets or assignment manipulate software program software, to record and screen your development. Regularly evaluate and examine your information, figuring out regions of improvement and celebrating milestones carried out.

Adapt and Refine

Goal placing is not a static technique; it requires model and refinement along the way. As you improvement, you may encounter new opportunities, challenges, or changes in instances. Be open to adjusting your desires if wished

Develop powerful verbal exchange abilties to connect to opportunities and team individuals

Effective communique skills are paramount in community advertising and marketing and advertising, as they permit you to connect authentically with prospects and construct robust relationships collectively in conjunction with your institution individuals. This summary explores the significance of growing effective communication abilities and offers realistic strategies to enhance your ability to connect, persuade, and encourage others for your network advertising and marketing adventure.

The Power of Effective Communication

Effective communication serves as the inspiration for fulfillment in network advertising. It permits you to supply your message clearly, set up rapport, and construct consider collectively together with your opportunities and organization participants. Effective communication lets in you to pay attention attentively, understand others' goals, and respond in a way that resonates with them. By growing strong communique competencies, you could create massive connections and strain the growth of your community advertising business.

Active Listening

Active listening is a essential element of effective communique. It includes in reality enticing with the speaker, giving them your undivided interest, and demonstrating proper hobby in what they have got to mention. Practice lively listening by using keeping eye contact, nodding to show facts, and asking clarifying questions. By actively listening, you now not best gain valuable insights into others' views and needs but additionally construct take delivery of as real with and rapport with them.

Develop Empathy

Empathy is the capability to understand and proportion the emotions of others. Cultivating empathy lets in you to connect on a deeper degree together with your opportunities and crew individuals. Put your self of their shoes, are searching for for to understand their annoying conditions and aspirations, and respond with compassion and statistics. By demonstrating empathy, you create a supportive and nurturing environment that fosters robust relationships.

Clear and Concise Communication

In network advertising and marketing, clean and concise communique is critical. Avoid the usage of jargon or technical terms which could confuse your target market. Use clean and easy language to carry your message effectively. Structure your communique in a logical manner, emphasizing key factors and the use of examples or testimonies to demonstrate your thoughts. By talking genuinely and concisely, you make certain that your message is with out problem understood and remembered.

Non-Verbal Communication

Non-verbal verbal exchange plays a terrific role in conveying your message. Pay interest for your frame language, facial expressions, and tone of voice. Maintain unique posture, make eye touch, and use suitable gestures to beautify your conversation. Project a assured and approachable demeanor , as it facilitates create a pleasing impact and fosters take into account and connection.

Adapt to Different Communication Styles

People have exclusive communication patterns, and adapting to the ones styles is critical for effective conversation. Some people select direct and concise communique, at the same time as others respect greater specific reasons. Observe and concentrate in your purpose market to apprehend their preferred fashion and adjust your communique as a result. Flexibility on your approach allows you to hook up with a broader form of human beings and assemble stronger relationships.

Practice Persuasive Communication

Persuasive conversation talents are treasured in community advertising and advertising. Learn to articulate the benefits and price of your products or services in a compelling manner. Highlight how they could address the dreams and desires of your possibilities. Use storytelling techniques, testimonials, and facts to useful resource your claims and create persuasive arguments. By studying persuasive communication, you can have an effect on others surely and encourage them to take action.

Conflict Resolution and Constructive Feedback

Conflict and disagreements are inevitable in any organization or enterprise environment. Develop skills in struggle decision and handing over nice feedback. Address conflicts right away and without delay, looking for win-win solutions that sell concord and growth. When presenting comments, be specific, recognition on behaviors , and offer guidelines for improvement. Constructive comments permits foster a way of lifestyles of non-stop reading and improvement.

Utilize Technology and Digital Communication Tools

In modern-day virtual age, leveraging technology and virtual conversation device is crucial. Utilize e mail, messaging apps, and social media structures to connect with your possibilities and organization individuals

Chapter 16: Embrace Non-Prevent Studying

In the ever-evolving global of community advertising, embracing non-stop gaining knowledge of and staying up to date on enterprise developments and techniques is crucial for success. This precis explores the significance of non-prevent studying and gives sensible techniques to help you extend your expertise, refine your skills, and stay at the leading edge of the employer.

The Value of Continuous Learning

Continuous studying is a thoughts-set that consists of looking for expertise and abilities beyond preliminary schooling. It permits you to conform to converting market dynamics, live in advance of the competition, and make knowledgeable choices in your community marketing and advertising and advertising agency. By embracing non-stop studying, you foster private increase, decorate your information, and role your self as a informed and dependable aid in your possibilities and crew participants.

Commit to Lifelong Learning

Make a willpower to lifelong gaining knowledge of with the useful resource of adopting a growth thoughts-set. Embrace the notion that there's constantly extra to examine and discover within the network advertising company. Develop a thirst for statistics and a hobby to find out new inclinations, strategies, and strategies. Approach every day as an opportunity to increase your knowledge and refine your abilities.

Stay Informed about Industry Trends

Network advertising and marketing is a dynamic area, with traits and super practices constantly evolving. Stay knowledgeable approximately enterprise dispositions via analyzing industry publications, following influential concept leaders, and attending meetings or webinars. Join relevant online corporations and participate in discussions to advantage insights from friends and organization experts. By staying abreast of agency developments, you may adapt your strategies and live in advance of the curve.

Engage in Continuous Training and Education

Take advantage of the training and academic sources to be had to you. Attend company organization-supplied schooling periods, webinars, and workshops to deepen your information and refine your capabilities. Seek out extra publications or certifications related to network advertising, manage, communique, or private development. Invest to your education and leverage those opportunities to growth your information.

Network with Industry Professionals

Networking with enterprise agency professionals is a treasured manner to have a look at from their reviews and advantage insights. Attend organization activities, meetings, and seminars to connect with like-minded human beings. Engage in meaningful conversations, ask questions, and share understanding. Build relationships with a fulfillment community entrepreneurs who can serve as mentors or assets of idea. Networking offers a wealth of reading opportunities and may open doors to collaboration and increase.

Leverage Online Learning Platforms

Online getting to know structures provide a sizeable form of guides and assets which could beautify your network advertising abilties. Explore structures which includes Udemy, Coursera, or LinkedIn Learning to get proper of entry to courses on topics which incorporates sales, advertising and advertising and marketing, conversation, or social media. These systems regularly provide flexibility, allowing you to analyze at your private pace and customise your studying journey.

Join Mastermind Groups or Peer Learning Circles

Mastermind agencies or peer mastering circles are small agencies of people who come collectively to percent records and guide every one-of-a-kind's increase. Join or shape a mastermind agency with fellow community marketers wherein you can speak disturbing conditions, change mind, and study from each different. Collaborative studying environments foster creativity, responsibility, and mutual boom.

Experiment and Test New Strategies

Continuous mastering consists of experimentation and trying out of new techniques. Be open to attempting current strategies, whether it's miles adopting new technologies, exploring one-of-a-kind marketing channels, or experimenting with revolutionary campaigns. Test and degree the effects to determine what works fantastic on your business employer. Embrace a mindset of continuous improvement, and use information and comments to refine your techniques.

Reflect and Evaluate Your Progress

Regularly reflect to your getting to know journey and take a look at your development. Take time to assess the effectiveness of the techniques you've got implemented, come to be privy to areas for improvement, and rejoice your achievements. Reflective exercise permits you to refine your approach, construct on successes, and studies from setbacks.

Find a great network advertising and marketing and advertising business corporation that aligns at the side of your values and gives tremendous services or products

When venturing into community advertising and marketing and advertising and marketing and advertising, selecting a good commercial enterprise business enterprise that aligns at the side of your values and gives great products or services is essential for prolonged-time period success. This summary explores the significance of choosing a reputable community marketing and advertising and marketing enterprise and offers practical techniques to help you take a look at and pick an company that meets your standards.

The Significance of Reputation

The popularity of a network advertising and marketing organisation is a reflected photograph of its credibility, integrity, and track record. A dependable organisation establishes recollect amongst its companies, customers, and the wider organization. Choosing a enterprise with a strong popularity no longer best enhances your personal credibility however additionally instills self assure in capability possibilities and crew humans.

Define Your Values and Priorities

Before exploring network advertising groups, take time to define your values and priorities. Consider the products or services that resonate with you for my part, further to those who align together with your ethical requirements and pastimes. Identify the values and standards which can be critical to you, which includes sustainability, social responsibility, or personal improvement. This readability will guide your search and make sure alignment with a employer that shares your values.

Research Potential Companies

Conduct thorough studies on capacity network advertising businesses. Explore their net net web sites, examine their project statements, and examine their product lines. Look for records approximately their agency history, management group, and their method to schooling and assist. Assess their reputation in the company with the useful resource of way of studying opinions, testimonials, and unbiased 1/three-party critiques. Utilize resources including enterprise courses, online forums, and social media corporations to collect insights from contemporary and former businesses.

Evaluate Product Quality and Market Demand

The nice of the products or offerings furnished via using a community advertising and marketing organisation is important for your achievement. Evaluate the extraordinary, area of knowledge, and market call for of the goods or offerings. Look for companies that prioritize studies and improvement, adhere to rigorous brilliant necessities, and provide products that provide genuine price to customers. Consider the marketplace developments and functionality for lengthy-time period boom in the commercial enterprise business enterprise.

Assess Compensation Plan and Income Potential

Evaluate the repayment plan supplied through way of the network advertising commercial enterprise organization. Assess the structure, charge fees, and bonuses to ensure they may be sincere and aligned together with your economic dreams. Look for transparency in how the repayment plan is communicated and recognize the incomes capacity based at the efforts required. Avoid companies that closely rely on recruitment with out a focal point on product income, as this will propose a pyramid scheme.

Consider Training and Support Systems

A legitimate network advertising and marketing agency will offer comprehensive schooling and manual structures that will help you be successful. Evaluate the property, gear, and education programs furnished by way of the company. Look for a strong onboarding manner, ongoing schooling possibilities, mentorship applications, and access to marketing materials. Assess the enterprise agency's dedication on your private and expert development.

Talk to Current Distributors

Engage with current-day agencies in the community marketing companies you are thinking about. Reach out to them for their firsthand memories and insights. Ask about their pleasure with the organization, the goods, the reimbursement plan, and the quantity of assist supplied. Listen to their recollections, successes, and annoying conditions. Their views will provide precious data that will help you make an knowledgeable selection.

Trust Your Instincts

After wearing out thorough studies and accumulating records, take delivery of as authentic together with your instincts on the identical time as making a totally closing choice. Consider how properly the enterprise company aligns on the facet of your values, the self guarantee you've got in its products or services, and the agree with you sense in the route of the leadership group. Choose a company that resonates with you on a private and professional degree, and in which you believe you can thrive and make a powerful effect.

Build a sturdy personal emblem to set up yourself as an expert for your niche

In the aggressive worldwide of network advertising and marketing, building a sturdy non-public emblem is critical to set up your self as an expert in your niche. This precis explores the significance of personal branding and gives realistic techniques to help you construct a effective and real private logo that resonates along with your aim marketplace.

Understanding Personal Branding

Personal branding entails the planned method of shaping and selling your particular identification, understanding, and values to distinguish your self from others. It is ready installing a strong and real presence that showcases your records, builds take into account, and attracts your audience. Developing a non-public brand lets in you to region yourself as an expert and influencer on your region of hobby.

Chapter 17: The Electricity of Social Media Structures to Extend Your Network

In cutting-edge virtual age, social media systems provide brilliant possibilities to community, be part of, and acquire a miles broader audience. This summary explores the significance of leveraging social media for community marketing and marketing and gives sensible techniques to help you make bigger your community and maximize your reap on those systems.

The Impact of Social Media on Network Marketing

Social media systems have revolutionized the way we be part of and speak. They offer a effective platform for community entrepreneurs to assemble relationships, share valuable content material fabric, and make bigger their achieve. Leveraging social media successfully lets in you to connect with a global target audience, have interaction with possibilities and business enterprise people, and set up your self as a depended on authority on your niche.

Identify the Right Social Media Platforms

Identify the social media structures which is probably most relevant in your goal market and align together with your network advertising and advertising and marketing goals. Popular structures which incorporates Facebook, Instagram, LinkedIn, Twitter, and YouTube provide particular features and demographics. Research the client demographics, engagement degrees, and types of content cloth that perform properly on each platform. Focus your efforts on the structures wherein your target market is most lively.

Optimize Your Social Media Profiles

Optimize your social media profiles to make a sturdy first have an impact on and entice your intention market. Use expert profile pictures, compelling cowl pictures, and interest-grabbing headlines. Craft a concise and attractive bio that highlights your information, values, and the blessings you offer. Include relevant key phrases and hashtags to your profiles to beautify discoverability. Make it clean for people to find out and hook up with you.

Consistency in Posting and Engagement

Consistency is fundamental whilst using social media for network advertising. Create a content cloth material calendar and expand a everyday posting time table. Regularly proportion treasured content fabric, together with informative articles, appealing movies, or inspiring fees, that align together together with your brand and resonate together together with your intention marketplace. Engage along side your aim marketplace through responding to feedback, messages, and inquiries proper away. Actively participate in applicable conversations, sharing your understanding and constructing relationships.

Use Visual Content to Capture Attention

Visual content cloth is pretty attractive and might seize the attention of your target audience on social media structures. Incorporate compelling photographs, pix, and movement photographs into your posts to influence them to visually attractive and stand out in crowded feeds. Use awesome visuals that replicate your emblem and communicate your message correctly. Experiment with unique formats, along with brief films, infographics, or stay streams, to diversify your content and maintain your goal marketplace engaged.

Leverage Hashtags and Keywords

Hashtags and key terms are powerful machine to boom your visibility and obtain on social media structures. Research and use applicable hashtags which is probably popular internal your location of interest and resonate together with your target market. Incorporate key terms strategically to your posts, profiles, and descriptions to beautify searchability. Engaging with trending hashtags and becoming a member of applicable conversations also can help expand your network and reach a far broader target audience.

Engage in Community Building

Community building is important for a success community marketing on social media. Create or be a part of applicable agencies, agencies, or forums in which your audience gathers. Actively take part in discussions, provide precious insights, and establish your self as a beneficial useful resource. Engage with influencers, concept leaders, and friends in your employer to assemble relationships and increase your network. Collaborate with others to host webinars, joint content cloth, or promotions to leverage every unique's networks.

Monitor and Analyze Metrics

Monitor and have a look at the metrics of your social media efforts to gain insights and enhance your approach. Track metrics along with reach, engagement, click on-through costs, and conversions. Use social media analytics device supplied with the aid of way of the usage of the systems or zero.33-party equipment to assess the overall performance of your content cloth and select out areas for improvement. Adjust your method based totally on the statistics to optimize your social media presence.

Utilize storytelling techniques to have interaction and captivate your target market

Storytelling is a effective tool that community marketers can make use of to engage and captivate their goal market. This precis explores the significance of storytelling in network advertising and marketing and advertising and gives realistic strategies to help you effectively include storytelling strategies into your marketing efforts.

The Power of Storytelling

Storytelling has been a critical part of human communication for masses of years. It has the potential to captivate emotions, create connections, and go away a long lasting impact. In community advertising, storytelling allows you to supply your logo message, encourage your target audience, and construct full-size relationships. By the use of storytelling strategies, you may have interaction your target audience on a deeper degree, making your message more memorable and compelling.

Understand Your Audience

Before crafting your tales, it is essential to apprehend your audience. Research their interests, aspirations, pain elements, and motivations. Identify the memories as a way to resonate with them and align with their values. By expertise your target marketplace, you can tailor your storytelling approach to seize their interest and create a substantial connection.

Craft a Compelling Narrative

A compelling narrative is the backbone of a effective story. Start by the use of way of defining the cause of your tale and the important issue message you need to preserve. Develop a shape that includes an creation, a conflict or mission, a climax, and a resolution. Use excellent and descriptive language to supply your story to lifestyles. Incorporate relatable characters, feelings, and conflicts that your audience can hook up with. This form will help your tale go with the flow seamlessly and have interaction your goal market from starting to prevent.

Share Personal Experiences

Sharing non-public reports is an powerful way to connect with your goal market on a deeper diploma. By sharing your very personal adventure, traumatic situations, and successes, you could create a experience of authenticity and relatability. Be inclined and apparent, as this permits your intention market to look the human aspect of your story. Personal reports help assemble accept as true with and credibility, making your purpose marketplace much more likely to connect with and spend money on your message.

Use Visual and Emotional Appeal

Visual and emotional attraction are essential factors in storytelling. Incorporate vibrant descriptions, sensory records, and imagery to colour a clear photograph in your goal marketplace's minds. Engage their emotions by manner of way of evoking emotions of pleasure, empathy, pleasure, or idea. Use metaphors, analogies, or anecdotes to simplify complex requirements and reason them to extra relatable. By appealing to each the visible and emotional senses, you can create a more immersive and impactful storytelling revel in.

Show the Transformation

One of the only elements of storytelling is showcasing transformation. Highlight how your product, provider, or opportunity has absolutely impacted the lives of others. Share testimonials, success reminiscences, and actual-lifestyles examples of human beings who have expert transformation thru your community advertising and advertising and marketing business enterprise. This allows your aim market envision themselves reaching similar outcomes, developing a experience of opportunity and motivation.

Incorporate Storytelling in Different Formats

Storytelling can be included in numerous codecs to cater to considered one of a type alternatives and structures. Use written testimonies in weblog posts, social media captions, or newsletters. Explore visible storytelling via films, pics, or infographics. Consider using live storytelling codecs which encompass webinars, podcasts, or stay streams. Adapt your storytelling style and format to in shape the specific platform and the alternatives of your target market.

Practice Active Listening

Active listening is a vital knowledge for powerful storytelling. Pay interest in your target marketplace's comments, feedback, and questions. Actively concentrate to their goals, desires, and disturbing situations. Incorporate their comments into your storytelling efforts to make sure relevance and resonance. Engage in conversations, ask open-ended questions, and display real hobby in your goal marketplace's stories. By actively listening, you may normally refine your storytelling method and offer content material cloth that truly connects with your target marketplace.

Foster relationships and offer rate on your network by way of the usage of way of providing useful property and resource

Building robust relationships and supplying value are critical elements of a success community advertising and marketing and marketing. This summary explores the importance of fostering relationships and presenting useful sources and help to your community. It gives practical techniques to help you cultivate large connections and come to be a precious useful resource to your community individuals.

The Power of Relationships in Network Marketing

Network advertising and advertising and marketing is constructed on relationships. Developing sturdy connections together together with your network contributors creates a enjoy of believe, loyalty, and mutual help. By nurturing these relationships, you may foster a fantastic and collaborative environment, leading to extended-term achievement. Building relationships isn't always pretty lots selling merchandise or recruiting crew individuals but approximately honestly being worried for and assisting others.

Cultivate a Genuine Interest in Others

To foster relationships, it is vital to cultivate a actual interest in others. Take the time to apprehend your community individuals' goals, demanding situations, and aspirations. Ask open-ended questions and actively listen to their responses. Show empathy, admire, and aid for their journey. By demonstrating a honest interest of their achievement, you create a strong foundation for constructing huge connections.

Provide Value Through Resources and Support

Providing price is the critical issue to turning into a precious resource for your community. Offer useful assets, equipment, and information that can help your community contributors in their personal and expert increase. Share academic content, education materials, and industry insights that align with their hobbies and desires. Provide steerage and manual thru mentoring, schooling, or ordinary check-ins. By presenting tangible fee, you set up yourself as a relied on representative and a person who actually wants to help others prevail.

Tailor Resources to Individual Needs

Recognize that each network member has particular desires and dreams. Tailor your property and guide to deal with their specific demanding situations and aspirations. Offer customized steering and hints based totally totally on their strengths and areas for improvement. Provide applicable education materials, articles, or webinars that might help them triumph over boundaries and advantage their goals. By customizing your support, you show your dedication to their man or woman success.

Create a Supportive Community

Foster a enjoy of network inner your network. Encourage collaboration, teamwork, and mutual guide among your community people. Facilitate possibilities for them to attach, percentage insights, and examine from each different. Create on-line companies, forums, or social media organizations wherein they could interact in discussions, ask questions, and offer assist. By fostering a supportive network, you provide a boost to relationships and enhance the overall community enjoy.

Be Responsive and Available

Availability and responsiveness are crucial in presenting help on your community. Be available and responsive for your community individuals' inquiries, issues, and requests for help. Respond to messages, emails, and calls straight away. Offer guidance and recommendation in a well timed manner. By being available and responsive, you construct receive as right with and exhibit your commitment to their achievement.

Share Success Stories and Testimonials

Success recollections and testimonials are effective gear to inspire and inspire your community members. Share tales of human beings who have finished achievement through your network advertising and marketing and advertising industrial company. Highlight their accomplishments, demanding situations they overcame, and the classes they determined out. These memories feature proof that success is achievable and offer guidance and concept to others in your network.

Encourage Personal Development and Growth

Support the private development and boom of your community people. Recommend books, podcasts, or guides that would extend their facts and abilities. Encourage them to set dreams, growth movement plans, and continuously strive for improvement. Provide encouragement and have fun their milestones and achievements. By fostering personal improvement and growth, you're making contributions to the general success of your network.

Chapter 18: Community with Like-Minded Specialists to Expand Your Connections

Attending industry sports and networking with like-minded professionals is a treasured method to growth your connections and beautify your community advertising efforts. This precis explores the significance of attending company activities and gives realistic pointers to help you make the most of those possibilities to extend your network.

The Importance of Industry Events

Industry sports provide a totally precise platform to connect with specialists on your subject, benefit industry insights, and stay up to date on the cutting-edge developments and tendencies. These activities supply collectively like-minded folks who share common hobbies and goals. By attending such occasions, you may assemble relationships, alternate thoughts, and collaborate with others to your corporation.

Research and Choose Relevant Events

Before attending agency events, behavior thorough studies to end up privy to those who align together with your place of interest, pastimes, and networking dreams. Consider elements which include the event's situation consider, aim market, and reputation. Look for activities that enchantment to employer professionals, idea leaders, and professionals you admire. Choose sports that offer academic instructions, workshops, and networking possibilities to maximize your enjoy.

Set Clear Objectives

Set easy goals for attending agency sports activities. Determine what you preference to attain, whether it's miles expanding your community, gaining understanding of new techniques, or finding capability collaborators or mentors. Having precise goals in thoughts will help you are making focused connections and make the maximum of it slow at the event.

Prepare Your Elevator Pitch

Craft a compelling elevator pitch to introduce yourself successfully at agency sports activities. Summarize who you are, what you do, and the rate you offer in a concise and appealing manner. Tailor your pitch to resonate along with your target audience and spotlight how you can benefit them. Practice delivering your elevator pitch with self notion and readability to make a strong impression whilst networking.

Engage in Meaningful Conversations

Networking at enterprise activities consists of carrying out significant conversations with fellow professionals. Approach others with a proper interest in their work and thoughts. Ask open-ended questions to inspire speak and actively take note of their responses. Share your non-public insights and evaluations even as being conscious of making a at the identical time beneficial exchange. Building proper connections via vast conversations can bring about extended-lasting relationships.

Utilize Social Media and Online Platforms

Leverage social media and online systems in advance than, at some point of, and after employer occasions to decorate your networking efforts. Connect with attendees and event organizers via structures together with LinkedIn, Twitter, or event-precise forums. Join relevant agencies and discussions to set up your presence and have interaction with employer specialists. During the occasion, percentage updates, insights, and images on social media, the use of event-unique hashtags to increase your obtain and connect with others.

Follow Up After the Event

The look at-up manner is crucial for nurturing and solidifying the connections made at company activities. Take the time to gain out to the professionals you met, whether or now not or no longer through custom designed emails, LinkedIn messages, or social media direct messages. Express your appreciation for the conversation and reference particular elements noted to reveal your right interest. Seek opportunities for similarly collaboration or examine-up discussions to maintain the momentum of the initial connection.

Stay Engaged with Industry Communities

Continue to stay engaged with enterprise businesses and networks past the occasion. Join online organizations, join applicable newsletters or blogs, and participate in webinars or digital meetups. Actively make a contribution to discussions, percent treasured content fabric, and provide assist to fellow experts. By staying engaged, you may nurture your connections, live updated on employer tendencies, and position your self as an energetic participant in your problem.

Develop management abilities and empower your group people to gain their dreams

Developing management abilities and empowering your crew people is vital in network advertising and marketing. This precis explores the significance of control in network advertising and advertising and offers sensible strategies that will help you turn out to be an powerful chief who empowers others to attain their goals.

The Role of Leadership in Network Marketing

Leadership plays a essential function in network advertising and advertising as it includes guiding and provoking a crew toward fulfillment. As a leader, you have got the responsibility to provide imaginative and prescient, path, and help to your group individuals. Effective control fosters a notable and empowering surroundings wherein individuals are inspired, recommended, and empowered to attain their complete functionality.

Lead thru Example

Leading by means of the usage of example is a essential problem of effective control. Model the behaviors and capabilities you want to look for your group participants. Demonstrate integrity, professionalism, and a sturdy art work ethic. Be proactive, reliable, and chargeable for your moves. By putting a powerful instance, you inspire your institution people to observe healthful and uphold immoderate requirements of performance.

Communicate Clearly and Effectively

Clear and powerful communique is critical for management in network advertising and marketing and advertising and advertising. Articulate your vision, desires, and expectancies in a concise and understandable way. Use active listening competencies to recognize your team participants' perspectives and troubles. Foster open and obvious communication channels, making sure that everyone feels heard and valued. Regularly offer remarks, guidance, and encouragement to facilitate increase and development.

Delegate and Empower

Effective leaders recognise the way to delegate obligations and empower their team members. Recognize the strengths and abilties of everybody and assign responsibilities consequently. Provide the essential sources, education, and help to permit them to achieve success. Trust your institution contributors to take ownership in their obligations and make choices. Empowering your group fosters a sense of ownership and obligation, important to improved motivation and productivity.

Foster a Collaborative Team Environment

Create a collaborative institution environment in which humans enjoy snug sharing mind, taking component, and supporting each other. Encourage teamwork, cooperation, and information sharing. Celebrate man or woman and group achievements, fostering a revel in of camaraderie and collective success. By promoting a collaborative surroundings, you create a supportive network that drives individual and group boom.

Chapter 19: Master the Artwork Of Comply With-As Much As Nurture Relationships

Mastering the artwork of take a look at-up is essential in network advertising and advertising as it lets in you to nurture relationships, construct bear in mind, and convert leads into reliable clients. This precis explores the significance of look at-up and offers realistic strategies that will help you effectively look at up with leads, preserve engagement, and ultimately gather success on your community advertising and marketing and advertising endeavors .

The Importance of Follow-up

Follow-up is a important issue of the income technique because it lets in you to live pinnacle of thoughts with capability clients and construct lasting relationships. Many leads require a couple of touchpoints earlier than they may be equipped to make a buy. Effective comply with-up helps you set up trust, cope with troubles, and provide extra information, in the end growing the hazard of changing leads into reliable customers.

Develop a Follow-up Strategy

Create a scientific and properly-described study-up approach to ensure consistency and effectiveness. Determine the frequency and timing of your look at-u.S. Of americabased on your target market and their alternatives. Consider the use of a mixture of verbal exchange channels, together with smartphone calls, emails, and social media messages, to acquire out to leads. Tailor your method to every person, taking into account their specific dreams and interests.

Personalize Your Follow-up

Personalization is high to a achievement test-up. Take the time to apprehend your leads' options, ache elements, and dreams. Use this statistics to craft customized messages that resonate with them. Address them via their call, reference previous conversations or interactions, and spotlight how your services or products can especially gain them. Personalized examine-up demonstrates your proper interest and care, growing the chance of a top notch response.

Provide Value in Every Interaction

Ensure that every examine-up interaction offers fee for your leads. Share relevant and beneficial facts, at the side of enterprise insights, suggestions, or property that align with their pursuits and desires. Offer solutions to their stressful conditions and show how your products or services can deal with their unique pain factors. By constantly imparting value, you function yourself as a relied on advertising and marketing representative and growth the opportunities of changing leads into customers.

Be Prompt and Responsive

Timeliness is vital in observe-up. Respond right away to inquiries, messages, or requests for information. Avoid retaining leads equipped, as it can cause frustration or lack of hobby. Demonstrate your professionalism and resolution via the use of being responsive and dependable. Quick and well timed follow-up indicates your dedication to assembly the desires of your leads and builds a immoderate excellent have an effect on of your emblem.

Use Automation and CRM Tools

Leverage automation and client dating control (CRM) equipment to streamline your comply with-up approach. Use e-mail autoresponders, drip campaigns, or chatbots to automate quality elements of your observe-up. CRM software permits you to track and control your leads, making sure that no observe-up opportunity falls thru the cracks. These system will let you live organized , maintain time, and offer a steady examine-up experience.

Be Persistent, Not Pushy

Persistence is crucial in follow-up, but it's far critical to strike the right balance and keep away from being pushy. Respect the limits and choices of your leads. If they particular disinterest or request to be contacted at a later time, honor their dreams. However, do not be discouraged through manner of preliminary rejections or loss of reaction. Continue to take a look at up in a polite manner and professionally, showcasing the price you could offer. Timing is vital, and your staying electricity may additionally additionally furthermore repay whilst leads are equipped to interact.

Monitor and Track Your Follow-up Efforts

Regularly display and music your study-up efforts to evaluate their effectiveness. Keep information of your interactions, which include key facts and effects. Analyze records, which includes reaction fees, conversion expenses, and consumer feedback, to understand styles and regions for improvement. Adjust your follow-up approach based totally on the insights won, optimizing your approach for higher outcomes.

Foster Long-Term Relationships

View comply with-up as an opportunity to foster lengthy-time period relationships together with your leads. Maintain normal verbal exchange even after a sale is made, as consumer retention is just as important as lead conversion. Continue to offer fee, offer beneficial resource, and preserve them updated on new merchandise or promotions. Building sturdy relationships encourages repeat purchases, referrals, and ongoing achievement for your network marketing commercial enterprise.

Continuously Improve Your Follow-up Skills

Keep honing your study-up competencies thru non-stop getting to know and development. Stay up to date on agency traits, profits techniques, and effective conversation strategies. Seek comments from leads and clients to gain insights into how you can beautify your take a look at-up technique. Embrace a growth attitude, continuously striving to beautify your look at-up talents and provide an wonderful client enjoy.

Utilize on-line tools and automation to streamline your techniques and maintain time

Utilizing on-line equipment and automation is essential in network advertising and marketing and advertising as it permits you to streamline your processes, growth performance, and save precious time. This precis explores the significance of leveraging on line gadget and automation and gives realistic techniques to help you optimise your workflow and gather achievement to your network advertising endeavors .

The Significance of Online Tools and Automation

Online equipment and automation play a crucial feature in community advertising via using simplifying duties, improving productivity, and enhancing commonplace overall performance. These equipment will will let you control various components of your commercial enterprise organization, which include lead generation, customer dating manage, social media advertising and marketing and advertising and marketing and marketing, and communication. By harnessing the strength of on line tools and automation, you may streamline your techniques, free up time, and interest on sports activities sports that pressure business enterprise increase.

Identify Your Business Needs

Start with the aid of way of figuring out your precise commercial company needs and pain factors. Determine which areas of your network advertising and marketing and advertising and marketing enterprise need to benefit from automation and on line tools. For instance, if lead technology is a project, you may keep in mind using lead seize paperwork or automated electronic mail advertising and marketing campaigns. By pinpointing your goals, you could successfully compare and choose the maximum appropriate tools to streamline your techniques.

Research and Evaluate Tools

Conduct thorough studies to apprehend the net equipment that align collectively along with your organisation necessities. There are numerous gear available, starting from purchaser relationship control (CRM) software application program to challenge control systems, social media schedulers, and electronic mail marketing and advertising and marketing solutions. Consider factors which incorporates capability, ease of use, price, and integration talents collectively together with your present structures. Read critiques, are trying to find hints, and take advantage of loose trials to make informed choices.

Automate Repetitive Tasks

Identify repetitive obligations on your network marketing and advertising agency that may be computerized. This can also include duties which include electronic mail take a look at-ups, social media posting, records entry, or lead nurturing. Explore automation system that let you time table and automate the ones responsibilities, saving you time and making sure consistency. Automation not pleasant will growth performance however additionally reduces the hazard of human mistakes.

Utilize Social Media Management Tools

Social media performs a extensive function in community marketing. Streamline your social media efforts by means of the usage of making use of social media control tools. These tools can help you time table posts in advance, reveal engagement, and have a look at performance. By the use of these system, you could preserve an active social media presence without spending immoderate time on guide posting and tracking.

Implement Email Marketing Software

Email marketing is an powerful approach in community advertising. Implement electronic mail advertising and marketing and advertising software program software software to automate your e mail campaigns, phase your goal marketplace, and track the performance of your emails. These device offer templates, personalization alternatives, and analytics to optimize your electronic mail marketing efforts. Automating your email campaigns saves time and permits you to nurture leads and gather relationships on autopilot.

Use CRM Software for Lead Management

A CRM (Customer Relationship Management) tool is critical for inexperienced lead manipulate. Implement CRM software application program to centralize and control your leads, track interactions, and display the development of your sales pipeline. CRM tools often embody abilties which includes touch manage, lead scoring, undertaking control, and reporting. By the use of CRM software application software program, you could streamline your lead manage approach, prioritize take a look at-ups, and improve conversion charges.

Leverage Project Management Platforms

If you decide with a collection or collaborate with others, leverage project manage systems to streamline verbal exchange, undertaking project, and improvement tracking. These systems let you assign obligations, set final dates, track milestones, and talk within a centralized tool. By the use of task manage system, you can enhance collaboration, enhance standard overall performance, and make sure everyone is aligned with mission dreams.

Integrate Tools for Seamless Workflow

Look for opportunities to integrate your on line system and systems to create a seamless workflow. For example, integrate your CRM device along with your e-mail advertising and marketing software to automate lead nurturing primarily based on specific triggers or actions. Seek tool that offer integration competencies or use 1/3-birthday celebration integrations to connect your structures. Integration removes guide records get entry to, minimizes mistakes, and enhances ordinary performance.

Stay Updated and Embrace New Technologies

Stay knowledgeable approximately new era and upgrades in on-line system and automation. The digital panorama is constantly evolving, and new gear are being superior frequently. Subscribe to relevant organisation courses, attend webinars or conferences, and participate in on-line organizations to stay updated. Embracing new generation permits you to stay in advance of the opposition and leverage the cutting-edge tools to streamline your procedures effectively.

Implement effective prospecting strategies to constantly enlarge your community

Implementing powerful prospecting strategies is vital in community marketing because it lets in you to constantly increase your community and enlarge your business enterprise. This summary explores the significance of prospecting and offers realistic techniques to help you choose out and connect with functionality leads, assemble relationships, and benefit achievement to your network advertising and marketing endeavors .

The Significance of Prospecting

Prospecting is the inspiration of network advertising and marketing. It involves actively seeking out and attractive with capability leads who may be inquisitive about your merchandise or employer possibility . Prospecting permits you to increase your community, construct relationships, and convert leads into customers or group people. It is a non-stop technique that fuels the boom and achievement of your community advertising and marketing and advertising commercial business enterprise.

Chapter 20: Advantage Treasured Insights and Steering

Seeking mentorship from professional community entrepreneurs is a precious technique which can extensively contribute for your success in the community advertising and advertising and marketing enterprise. This summary explores the importance of mentorship and gives sensible insights at the manner to find out and leverage mentor relationships to gain treasured guidance and insights that may propel your community advertising and marketing and advertising and marketing profession.

The Importance of Mentorship

Mentorship performs a vital position in private and professional improvement. In community advertising and advertising, having a mentor can provide you with steering, assist, and treasured insights gained through their personal reports. A mentor can provide a glowing mindset, percentage employer-specific data, and help you navigate traumatic conditions, in the long run accelerating your increase and achievement.

Identify Potential Mentors

Begin with the aid of way of figuring out capability mentors inside the community advertising enterprise. Look for individuals who've completed fulfillment and really own the expertise and expertise you are looking for. This might be someone inside your very own community marketing and advertising commercial enterprise agency or specialists outside of it. Consider attending company events, meetings, or networking companies to connect with professional community entrepreneurs who can likely become your mentor.

Build Genuine Relationships

Building actual relationships with ability mentors is essential. Approach them with apprehend and a real desire to research from their opinions. Take the time to set up rapport, show interest of their adventure, and exhibit your strength of will to personal increase. Building a robust basis primarily based totally on believe and mutual apprehend increases the possibility of a a fulfillment mentorship relationship.

Clearly Define Your Goals and Expectations

Before drawing close a functionality mentor, in truth define your dreams and expectancies. Understand what you wish to gain from the mentorship and articulate it correctly. This clarity will not high-quality help you perceive the right mentor however additionally permit your mentor to understand how they will be capable of useful aid you effectively. Clearly speaking your goals sets the inspiration for a useful mentorship relationship.

Seek a Variety of Perspectives

Consider looking for mentorship from people with severa perspectives and evaluations. This can provide you a broader sort of insights and processes to network marketing. Look for mentors who've completed success in exquisite niches or markets, or who own precise abilities or techniques. Having get proper of access to to numerous views can beautify your capacity to conform, innovate, and thrive inside the dynamic community advertising landscape.

Be Open to Feedback and Constructive Criticism

A key component of mentorship is receiving feedback and positive criticism. Be open and receptive to comments out of your mentor, as it is an possibility for boom and development. Embrace the mentor's insights and suggestions, no matter the fact that they venture your contemporary beliefs or practices. Being open to feedback demonstrates your willingness to analyze and evolve, positioning you for extra success.

Leverage the Mentor's Knowledge and Network

Tap into the mentor's statistics and network to increase your private possibilities. Engage in discussions, ask questions, and are trying to find advice on severa components of network marketing and advertising and marketing. Your mentor can offer treasured enterprise-particular facts, percentage a success strategies, and introduce you to their network, collectively with capability leads or collaborators. Leverage the mentor's expertise and connections to enhance your private network advertising and advertising efforts.

Take Action and Implement Mentor's Advice

A mentor's guidance is valuable best whilst placed into movement. Actively follow the insights and recommendation furnished through way of your mentor. Implement their techniques, test new strategies, and have a observe the outcomes. Consistent movement is prime to translating mentorship into tangible consequences. Be accountable to your self and your mentor, regularly reporting your progress and on the lookout for in addition steering as wanted.

Nurture the Mentor Relationship

Mentorship is a -manner street. Show gratitude for the time and know-how shared through your mentor. Nurture the connection with the useful aid of keeping everyday conversation, imparting updates on your development, and expressing appreciation for his or her assist. Share your successes and annoying conditions, and trying to find ongoing guidance as your network marketing journey unfolds. A robust mentor courting can evolve into an extended-time period expert connection or maybe a collaboration possibility.

Pay It Forward

As you advantage enjoy and knowledge in community marketing, endure in mind paying it forward with the beneficial aid of becoming a mentor your self. Share your information and insights with others who're starting their journey. Mentorship is a cyclical way, and contributing to the increase of others now not exceptional advantages them however moreover reinforces your very own understanding and reinforces your function as a respected employer expert.

Embrace resilience and take a look at from failures to fuel your boom

Embracing resilience and getting to know from disasters is critical for personal and expert growth, specifically in the dynamic assignment of network advertising and advertising and marketing. This summary highlights the significance of resilience, explores the thoughts-set had to navigate setbacks, and gives practical strategies to turn disasters into treasured reading possibilities.

The Power of Resilience

Resilience is the capability to get higher from demanding situations, setbacks, and disasters. In community marketing and advertising, wherein rejection and limitations are commonplace, resilience is a key trait that fuels boom and fulfillment. Embracing resilience permits you to hold a great mind-set, persevere in the face of adversity, and studies from setbacks to in the long run reap your dreams.

Cultivate a Growth Mindset

Developing a increase attitude is important with reference to embracing resilience. A boom attitude is the belief that intelligence, competencies, and abilities can be advanced via determination, try, and non-prevent mastering. Embrace disturbing conditions as opportunities for increase, view disasters as getting to know critiques, and trust on your potential to enhance. Adopting a growth mind-set empowers you to appearance setbacks as brief and broaden the resilience wanted to triumph over them.

Shift Your Perspective on Failure

Change your angle on failure thru viewing it as a stepping stone to achievement as opposed to a totally final final consequences. Failure is not a meditated photo of your properly really worth or abilities, but as an alternative an opportunity to research and expand. Embrace disasters as valuable comments, extract commands from them, and use those classes to refine your strategies and techniques. By moving your attitude, you could rework disasters into stepping stones towards greater fulfillment.

Analyze and Learn from Failures

Take the time to test and replicate in your failures. Identify what went wrong, the factors that contributed to the failure, and the schooling you could extract from the revel in. This self-reflection permits you to gain insights into your strengths and weaknesses, understand regions for improvement, and alter your technique transferring in advance. Learning from failures is a vital step toward private and expert boom.

Seek Feedback and Support

Don't be afraid to are attempting to find feedback and guide from mentors, colleagues, or team individuals. They can provide treasured insights, opportunity perspectives, and positive grievance. Feedback allows you find out blind spots, discover regions for development, and refine your strategies. Surrounding yourself with a supportive community of those who remember for your functionality can bolster your resilience and offer steering for the duration of hard instances.

Maintain a Positive Mindset

Maintaining a extraordinary mind-set is vital whilst handling failures and setbacks. Focus at the classes discovered in choice to residing on the terrible elements. Practice gratitude, have fun small wins, and visualize your achievement. By cultivating a extraordinary mindset, you could navigate demanding situations with optimism, maintain motivation, and get higher stronger from setbacks.

Chapter 21: Rewards to Inspire Your Group Individuals

Offering incentives and rewards is a powerful technique to inspire and incentivize group people within the network advertising company. This precis highlights the significance of motivation in network advertising and advertising and marketing and marketing, explores the benefits of offering incentives and rewards, and offers realistic tips for implementing an powerful incentive software program.

The Role of Motivation in Network Marketing

Motivation plays a essential position in the success of network advertising and marketing organizations. When group individuals are inspired, they're much more likely to set and reap their goals, live devoted to their company, and actively make a contribution to the general achievement of the group. By offering incentives and rewards, you may create a lifestyle of motivation and foster a sense of success among your group contributors.

Benefits of Offering Incentives and Rewards

Offering incentives and rewards has numerous benefits in community advertising. Firstly, it boosts morale and creates a effective paintings surroundings, main to extended productiveness and engagement. Secondly, incentives and rewards recognize and appreciate the efforts and achievements of institution members, which permits gather loyalty and retention. Additionally, incentives can lure new crew participants and encourage them to enroll in and perform at their tremendous. Overall, an powerful incentive software program can electricity motivation, beautify group common overall performance, and contribute to the general achievement of your network advertising and marketing industrial corporation.

Define Clear and Attainable Goals

Before implementing an incentive software, it's miles critical to outline smooth and conceivable dreams. Clearly talk the desires or milestones that group people need to benefit so that you can qualify for incentives or rewards. Ensure that the goals are realistic, measurable, and aligned with each individual and group goals. When desires are clean and conceivable, crew contributors are more likely to stay induced and art work in the direction of reaching them.

Offer a Variety of Incentives and Rewards

To cater to the numerous options and motivations of your company members, offer an entire lot of incentives and rewards. Consider monetary rewards, along with bonuses or commissions, in addition to non-financial rewards, along with reputation, offers, or unique studies. Personalize the incentives primarily based totally on character options each time possible. Providing numerous incentives and rewards will increase the appeal and motivation for organization contributors, as they are capable of choose the rewards that resonate with them the most.

Regularly Communicate and Reinforce Incentive Program

Effective conversation is essential to the success of an incentive utility. Clearly speak the facts, necessities, and timelines of the program to all crew participants. Regularly remind them of the incentives and rewards they will be able to earn and replace them on their development. Use a couple of communication channels, which includes institution meetings, e mail newsletters, or on-line structures, to make certain that the incentive application stays pinnacle-of-thoughts and encourages active participation.